Just Champion!
Alex Ferguson
with Peter Fitton

"For Cathy, Mark, Jason, Darren and my brother Martin
for their unfailing support, the hard-working staff at the club,
and the loyal supporters that helped make
Manchester United true champions."

An official publication of Manchester United Football Club

Just Champion!
Alex Ferguson
with Peter Fitton

Peter Fitton
is The Sun's leading Northern sportswriter. He has covered all United's major games
at home and abroad for more than 20 years after a sporting graduation on the Stretford End.
His journalistic duties have also taken him to the finals of three World Cups and European
championships. Outside business hours, Peter occupies his time with cricket,
golf and sailing his boat.

Photography

John Peters: *cover; pages 3, 28, 34-9, 62, 66, 73-5, 79, 80, 84, 106, 112-121, 125-6, 130, 148*

Action Images: *pages 13, 15, 22, 24, 33, 40, 42, 44, 46, 48, 51, 54, 56, 57, 58, 60, 63, 67, 68, 69, 72, 83, 86, 89, 91-2, 94, 97-99, 101-3, 109, 123, 136, 141-2, 145, 147*

Allsport: *pages 10, 14, 64, 76, 78, 85, 93, 96, 135; back cover*

Empics: *pages 20, 78-9, 104, 142*

Sportsview: *page 108*

Published by Manchester United Football Club plc
Old Trafford, Manchester, M16 0RA

First Published 1993

ISBN 0 952 0509 1 9

Printed and bound in Great Britain by Stephens & George
Reprographics by Essex Reprographics

CONTENTS

"Suddenly you're a champion.
Sit back, absorb the experience,
soak up the pleasure -
and smile a while."

CHAPTER ONE

The Magic Roundabout

The afternoon of May 2nd, 1993 when we were crowned the champions of England, was the day I truly became manager of Manchester United. Exactly six years and 177 days after I was officially appointed to the job.

It might be a strange, even perplexing statement to make, with European and domestic success already on my Old Trafford record. But, for me anyway, it was the historic moment when I could finally realise, even inwardly accept for the first time, that I was the man in charge. There was a sudden, overwhelming realisation that now I was master of my own destiny.

Nobody can ever again have ultimate power at United. The dimension of the club is too vast to make that possible. It's beyond the scope of a single human being, no matter how impressive or gifted. But, at least on the football side of the business, I could sit back and plan the next five years of United's future. And at last be comfortable in the knowledge that I could carry it through to a conclusion. Until that fancy bit of silverware was in our grasp nothing could be taken for granted, nothing was ever that certain or clear.

Of course, even without the title, I had mapped out the seasons ahead. Although it was always with fingers crossed and a private prayer that I would still be secure, still perched in the manager's chair, still around to put my plans into practice. The championship triumph, apart from ending 26 years of collective cursing and frustration, was unquestionably the breaching of a barrier that had defied so many talented people, world renowned players as well as managers. It was the great dividing line. In an instant my professional horizons changed. I had booked my spot. I wasn't ever fearful of the sack, but winning the League meant there was no longer a threat looming over my work. The burden of history had been lifted from the shoulders of everybody.

I could feel, at last, like Arnold Palmer marching down a fairway of acclaim towards victory in The Open. No kidding, that's what it felt like. What had been a little fantasy of mine at the start of the wackiest, craziest, most wonderful 24 hours of my life, was about to come true. It was the day when we won the greatest prize of all without even kicking a ball.

Aston Villa, Ron Atkinson's team and our most dedicated pursuers for most of the season, needed to beat Oldham Athletic at home to stay in the race. Live to the nation, the great showdown to determine our fate was on the box. I decided I could do without it. Fergie the football fanatic was off to the golf course instead.

Aye, at best a 20-handicap hacker, I preferred to join eldest son Mark just a mile or two up the road from home at the Mottram Hall course. It was during the morning work-out session with the team that I decided it would make sense if the big game being screened from Villa Park was placed on the boys' banned list. It was pointless being upset by events beyond our control - giving it the button was the only sensible option. I suspected it might leave us all in a state of turmoil, and I told the players it was absolutely taboo in my house. I was off playing golf and suggested they do the same.

To be perfectly honest, when I arrived in the locker-room at the golf course I quietly questioned what I was doing. Was I in the wrong place at the right time? It was 1.50 pm when we started playing. For the first few holes I didn't feel all that good. My chest was heavy and tight. Should have stayed by the box after all, I figured. A touch of nerves, maybe the long-distance title twitch. Mark noticed I was uncomfortable but advised me to stop worrying about Villa. I did and by the sixth, thanks to the generosity of a shot a hole, I was three in front. Ten holes later with another half on the card, I couldn't fail.

The seventeenth tee allows you to scan right across the wide, flat Cheshire plain to Manchester's high rise skyline. Nice view - pity about the result I thought, as I dumped my drive straight into the lake on the left.

"Villa must have won by now," muttered Mark, "otherwise somebody would have been out to tell us." I nodded and knocked another ball up the fairway.

Then I spotted a stranger in a car eyeing us up. He stopped, then started reversing along the tree-lined driveway, but by this time we were on the green. Mark ran one past and I was hunched over the old putter when I sensed footsteps thudding up behind me.

"Mr. Ferguson?" he asked and, before I could even answer, he beat me to it, blurting out, "They murdered Villa... Oldham have won... It's all over... United are champions!" Bedlam. I thought he was joking but Mark was climbing all over me with a bear hug of congratulation. Minutes later it was confirmed by another supporter, our ex-Catering Manager Jim Barker's son. Needless to say we didn't play the eighteenth.

Normally that fairway home to the clubhouse takes seven or eight minutes to walk. I floated down it, head in the clouds, in a matter of what seemed like five seconds. And all the way my mind drifted back to another triumph, on a very different golf course, more than thirty years earlier. I had been at Troon in 1961 when the great Arnie Palmer won the Open. I watched his every step down the last that day with the crowds hollering his name and worshipping his achievement. I don't mind admitting I slipped into my own fantasy world on May 2nd 1993, and felt just like Arnie must have done. Like a gladiator coming home.

The dream was only broken by a bunch of four Japanese golfers just in front. All afternoon they had held us up, totting up the yardages and measuring putts. Go-slow golf, otherwise we would have been home to catch the final minutes of the Villa game. One of them, I noticed, was wearing a Manchester United cap. He had to be let into the big secret.

"We're the champs," I shouted across. In reply came a chorus of "ah-so" and not much else. Mark fell about laughing.

"Well, that went down a bundle, dad," he said. I left the fairway feeling totally stupid, a complete wally. The most embarrassed champion England has probably ever seen; a face as red as a United shirt. But not for long.

As soon as we pulled into the drive we realised we were not alone. People were piling into the house from every direction. My butcher, a big Reds' fan, was soon knocking on the door with four of his pals. The chairman, Martin Edwards, rolled up with the champers. And not long after came the car-loads of supporters. A father and son, somebody I had never met before, were soon in the house. Both wearing sweatshirts with the logo, "Fergie's Premier League Champs '93." Almost before big Ron was able to realise he and Villa had failed my folks were pouring in from Scotland.

A swinging night

It was a swinging night. A wonderful, dancing, celebrating, huggin' and kissin' night until I called it a draw about half past two. No sleep, impossible really, the mind racing with so many thoughts and the feeling that I couldn't get down to Old Trafford fast enough. Up at seven and then hanging around until after lunch. The Blackburn kick-off wasn't until evening.

Inevitably I was in a restless mood. I couldn't grab the papers fast enough, catching them as they dropped through the letter box. I needed to be sure that it was true, that I wasn't dreaming. But there was no chance of that. The phone was drilling a hole in my head. It never stopped ringing. For a spell I thought the whole planet had been given my number. Then, finally, freedom. I was heading for the place I most wanted to be.

But when I reached the ground, nudging the car slowly forward through the crush, it was simply incredible. Just a swaying, laughing, jostling mass of people. Thousands of United followers filling the forecourt. They slapped my back, roared my name, and thanked me for the championship. Honestly, at that moment I felt our roles should have been reversed. I should have been thanking them. Think about it. Every season since 1967 another chance of winning the title had been lost. Every summer a new signing arrived. Every August there was the sense of expectation, the vain hope that at long last the final piece of the jigsaw was about to fall into place. But never, in the depths of frustration and disillusionment, did the dream die. Never, with so much failure to suffer, did the overwhelming belief disappear that one day United would be champions again.

Imagine the emotional and financial costs of the crusade. The dedicated follower had probably parted with thousands upon thousands of pounds to see the team attain the Holy Grail. Not to mention the families that had been split apart, the mothers' hearts that were broken, the marriages that have ended prematurely - all in the name of that elusive prize. Yes, they had earned every second of their soccer party.

But while they swopped tales of a season's special memories, I sneaked off by myself to prepare for Kenny Dalglish's team. I slid into a seat in the empty main stand. The place was like a cathedral, so atmospheric. The carnival, in all its colours of flags and banners, was not far away. It was, as I knew it would be, a sensational night. You work all your life to hit such a peak of excitement, the pinnacle of your career; yet it disappears so quickly. You can't package it, hold on to the magic of it. If you could, you would live past a hundred in expectation of something special and never be bored. Normally the final whistle is my moment of success or failure. The game then drains away very quickly. But the championship night could have gone on for eternity. I just didn't want it to end. For once I could have been tempted to hire one of those time-warp machines from Star Trek.

Steve Bruce already had his own *Captain's Log*, a special in-house video of the title run-in being made for TV. He had been toting the camcorder with him for a couple of months. He was our own Jeremy Beadle, capturing the daft, crackpot moments as well as the treasured memories of a campaign that had tested the resolve and nerve of everybody involved. Brucie had phoned me just as I arrived back from the golf course. Was it okay, he asked, if the players had a few beers, just one or two, you understand, to toast the title achievement, even though they were preparing for Blackburn. They were all gathered at his house, anyway, and he just wanted the nod of approval.

In most circumstances, I would have said no way, the night before a big game.

But this time it was special, so, with the warning not to go crackers, I told Brucie and the boys to get on with it. I cautioned them, however. We still had to meet a stadium full of fans and we shouldn't make fools of ourselves. When I saw the video later, it appeared the beer or two had turned into a loaded dray of the stuff!

Let's just say they were fairly relaxed when they arrived at the ground a couple of hours before kick-off. They came in dribs and drabs. I was waiting for them all in one of Old Trafford's restaurants. As you can guess it was very emotional. But soon I could hear all the tittle-tattle among the players about exactly what went on the night before. I tried to shut my ears to it all. I'm a stickler for pre-match discipline and, really, I just didn't want to know. I didn't dare ask... it was better I didn't have the details of their partying. Whether they had swigged a beer or two too many and been forced to their beds. But I got the drift about what had happened to Lee Sharpe. As soon as Lee heard the Villa result, he piled into a car with his father and headed down to the ground. Already the place was swinging. He was practically dragged from the car and in seconds was shoulder high being carried the whole way round the stadium by a seething mass of supporters. Fabulous experience for him. I just wish I had thought about it and dropped in. He ended up dancing the night away with the fans outside Old Trafford.

You can understand those supporters. They have suffered so much frustration and their long-enduring patience is hard to believe. Their sense of relief, their need to celebrate was the most natural thing in the world. And I could also forgive the players, no matter what their celebration antics had been. For any footballer at the club the strain of pursuing the championship has been enormous. Just flick back through the memory bank and consider the heroic figures of the past who tried and failed to destroy the jinx. Forget the Busby era and simply reflect on the world-class operators since the late sixties. They roll off the tongue: Arnie Muhren, Joe Jordan, Norman Whiteside, Paul McGrath, Gordon Strachan... The list is endless. For 25 years the United record is littered with outstanding individuals who gave everything and never quite made it.

So you don't need a masters' degree to imagine the elation that poured from our players when they managed to burst through the barrier. It could only be measured on the Richter scale. When you achieve something special, predictably I suppose, you relax your discipline. And for a few madcap hours we all did that.

I had photographers up at my house all night. Very pleasant bunch they were, too. But, in most cases, people invading my privacy at home are guaranteed one instant response: a boot up the backside. For a time the barricades were down. The same crew were waiting in ambush down at the ground. To help edition times they wanted me to pose with the Premier League trophy before the game kicked off. No bother. But I could hardly believe the piece of silverware in front of me. Twenty three pounds in weight and a little ostentatious. What you might call OTT. But who was complaining? Not me. If it had been an empty bean can with the maker's name ripped off and 'Champions' engraved instead, it would have been the most beautiful thing on earth to me. Give me more - I would take one a season for the next ten years. The one we collected, though, brand new

Twenty three pounds of silverware

and shimmering, could never in a hundred years be more deservedly earned.

The true hallmark of United's footballing quality was underlined when it mattered most. The last seven games turned into The Magnificent Seven - the sort of victory roll few managers can ever expect.

"The last manager to do that here," chided our director Mike Edelson, "got the sack." I laughed. But I knew he was right. It was Dave Sexton in the seventies and it's a statistic that demonstrates how unfair football can be.

But justice, soccer-style, was very much on our side. Because these particular United champions didn't merely conquer the rest, they also played with a conviction, rhythm and potency that few could match. The fixture with Villa was a classic of its kind. A tremendous banner-carrier for our business. It wasn't just the artistry and skill but, more important, the spirit of the contest. There was nothing nasty in the whole game, nobody trying the rough stuff to intimidate or sort out a rival. A tackle, hard and painful maybe, didn't provoke those chest-to-chest showdowns you see so often these days. And considering what was at stake it was highly commendable. In the end, the result was all-square, but in my mind that wasn't quite the equation. It taught me what I always suspected: we were essentially the better team. And that conclusion was so important as we got closer and closer to the wire.

After the game, I told the players: "You slaughtered them. They should go down on their knees to the 'keeper - he earned them a point." Even then I had my calculations carefully worked out. On a flying trip to New York, planning some future coaching work, I made the chairman a promise. If we finished March hovering a point or two from the summit, we would be champions. I had worked out a rough script of how the season would play out if we got to that point, and although we were upstaged now and again, I was very happy with how we hogged the limelight in the final act. I always figured Villa might come unstuck at Blackburn. And, of course, they did.

Destiny fulfilled

To be honest, in the closing phase, I was never really too concerned about what I suddenly envisaged as our destiny. Fate had wrecked us the year before. Not this time. I wasn't looking for any more breaks after the Sheffield Wednesday game at Old Trafford. Think back - I'm sure you recall the situation. A goal down with the desperate final minutes ticking away. Villa had already been held to a goal-less draw by Coventry and were in the bath. Even so, they couldn't have been more hot and bothered than our boys. Then Steve Bruce equalised. Into overtime, plenty of it as well. And Brucie is there again. Two-one, victory against the odds, and as fateful a twist in the title dialogue of two teams as anyone could have imagined. Seven-and-a-half minutes of added time and eyebrows throughout the nation were raised. I've meticulously checked the video, and I can tell you without a shadow of doubt it should actually have been twelve. Everybody forgets the long delay when the referee Michael Peck was crocked and had to leave the field.

But through all that drama and tension, with Brian Kidd sliding knees first on to the pitch and reaching to the heavens, I am now left with one never-to-be-forgotten picture. The central character? Who else but Bryan Robson? Cast your mind back to the split-second when Brucie's header was looping on to the target. Aye, sure enough, there was Robson, his eyes laser-gripped to the ball, watching it arc into the goal and then smash Wednesday defender Nigel Worthington - himself guarding the line - into oblivion. He wasn't being nasty or malicious, just showing the commitment and defiance of a man born to win. He did exactly the same against QPR, swallowing his tongue and ending up in a hospital bed. Close to tragedy then, it never stopped him risking every bone in his body, again and again. That, if I can underline it simply, is what makes him a legend to rest comfortably alongside the likes of Bobby Charlton and George Best. That streak of devilment, a combination of courage and sheer bloody-mindedness. It doesn't come in bottles, more's the pity, and mercifully the boys had recovered from what they downed in theirs as they rolled up for the Blackburn jamboree.

Bryan Robson - "born to win"

The soccer calendar hadn't turned up with much of a deal for Dalglish's team, I must admit, sending them to our place on such a special night. Blackburn hadn't a prayer. The whole world was against them even though all they wanted was a place in Europe after a season of too many broken ambitions. Apart from that there was no point to their exercise, and it showed. Admittedly, they scored a goal and, particularly in the first half, put themselves around with real aggression in midfield. But once we had shaken free of the cobwebs - or was it the celebration champagne? - it was a bit like the last waltz. Not quite, I suppose, because waiting at chucking-out time in the final game were, of all the party-poopers in the land, shy and retiring Wimbledon. Beetle-crushers and all.

They could wait, as far I was concerned. The important issue was the crowning of the champions and who was to wear the crown first. The speculation centred obviously on Brucie, skipper for most of the season, and our long-term captain Robbo. It was a sweetly simple decision for me. It had to be the pair of them in tandem. Steve would be the last person on the planet to deny Bryan the glory he has earned in so many seasons of self-sacrifice. I always knew that the presentation debate outside the club was never going to be an issue inside Old Trafford. That done, another drink or two with Simply Red's Mick Hucknall down below in a suddenly quiet dressing-room, off for a champagne breakfast at two in the morning, and flakers. The adrenalin tank was running on empty and didn't I know it. Bed was the only answer, even if I accepted there might still be a nightmare waiting at Wimbledon.

*Coping
with the
Crazy Gang*

My fear wasn't ever focused on the possibility of losing to them. On the football field I never worried that we couldn't cope. The real concern, which I deliberately shielded at the time, was the inevitable hype we could expect from a team that never stops gloating on their reputation as the Crazy Gang. They didn't let me down. I knew it would be plastered in all the papers that Wimbledon weren't in the business of paying respects to the new champions. The party was over, they warned, and we could expect them to walk right over the top of us and leave us sprawled on the deck. We have heard it all before and I don't expect it will ever stop. It's part of that club's culture. My message to the United players was not philosophical or fancy. I reminded them of what was necessary. Just let's prove how strong the champs are by winning the game - in style. Let me say they are nowhere near as bad as they used to be, but they have brought back Vinnie Jones and, just occasionally, unfortunate things happen.

One did, in the first minute. Vinnie came flying in with an absolutely ridiculous tackle on Paul Ince. Really, he should have been sent off for it. The challenge was so late I think the Jones boy only thought of it by Monday - and this game was being played Sunday. But Incey had the perfect answer. He climbed to his feet and just laughed in Vinnie's face. It was absolutely the attitude we needed in our crowning moment. We had already demonstrated throughout the season we were a team of football quality; now this was the classic opportunity to underpin United's development as an outfit of courage and substance. We needed to compete, show real style - not go under to any intimidation. I believe we did exactly that. Not just to the sporting public in general but to that vast army of away-day followers that played such a crucial role of their own in the winning game. I'll never forget how they trekked to the south London outpost of Selhurst Park, for the victories over Crystal Palace and Wimbledon, in their thousands, twice in 18 days. Two lock-outs, with fractionally more than 62,000 witnessing epic achievements, was unbelievable, particularly with the realisation that more than 40,000 of them were our own long-distance

"You work all your life to hit such a peak of excitement, the pinnacle of your career; yet it disappears so quickly."

travellers. I don't think I'll ever see that kind of support at that ground again in my lifetime. The response of our fans was simply mind-blowing.

And 'Dons owner Sam Hammam was generous to a fault. He loaded champagne into our dressing-room and helped us celebrate. Also, a few weeks previously, he had shown the other face of Wimbledon with a letter of congratulations after our Youth team beat their kids in the cup.

Just as stunning in its impact on the old brain cells is, of course, the realisation that a thousand days of frustration and torment, exhilaration and despair, are over. Suddenly, you are a champion. Sit back, absorb the experience, soak up the pleasure - and smile a while. It's like being on the magic roundabout.

You don't want to ever fall off, either. The ride is too good. There is in all human beings that inborn sense of pride and self-satisfaction. In a way you start preening yourself and, with a little show of personal indulgence, maybe drop into the clever-boy syndrome. Not that you have cracked it in securing the title but that you have beaten history as well as the Premier League opposition. All those outstanding managers, all those gifted players that United have had down the generations, all the challengers who just failed to wrap their fingers around the prize. You think about them, of course you do. And then you think that, finally, after huge financial investment and a massive show of commitment, you have done it. The obsession is over. It's been conquered. Now let's have another one.

So many other contenders, I appreciate, might have beaten me to it. There was, and I'm sure United followers won't ever forget, Wilf McGuinness taking on the very demanding responsibility of being Sir Matt Busby's successor in the late sixties. When he took charge he still had great players surrounding him. In roughly eighteen months, Wilf led United to five semi-finals. At some football institutions not far from here that would have assured him a job for life. But he didn't win the League, the ultimate judgement on everybody at Old Trafford, and he disappeared through the door.

Past masters

Next Frank O'Farrell who brought Martin Buchan to United and with him the defensive style and iron will of a Bobby Moore. Then the Doc, Tommy Docherty of course, with his swaggeringly brash team of entertainers that included Lou Macari and Stuart Pearson - two relatively cheap acquisitions - plus Jimmy Greenhoff and the home-developed Sammy McIlroy. Even nowadays many folk think the Doc was absolutely wonderful for United. For pity's sake! He got us relegated. How can you be hero-worshipped for that? And it wasn't in his first season, either, but his second. The bottom line to his popularity was dramatically simple. He had an image of the buccaneering boss, a man of the people if you like. Docherty always cultivated the media - his code seemed to be that fair exchange was no robbery, and they were quite happy to play along with him. Two Cup Finals, no title, and Tommy was off over the horizon. His replacement was Dave Sexton. The complete opposite, you might say, and a manager who had the total respect of his contemporaries and players.

Dave Sexton - "had the total respect of his contemporaries and players."

Dave's knowledge of the game was unchallenged, his coaching methods universally taken on board by others and admired. He knew how to behave in the football profession and strictly obeyed very strong principles across all areas of his life. And let me remind you one more time that he won his last seven games of the season before being sacked. Not always a fair world, is it?

Ron Atkinson, my immediate predecessor, was the next brave man to pop his head out of the trench and into the firing line. He dodged the bullets for almost six years and claimed a fair amount of valuable territory in the process. Big Ron was never too far away from the major awards, always top four in the championship chase, and in charge of the dream team that had a nation in disbelief with ten straight wins. Wembley was like his second home. Six times in three years he made the trip in various Cup competitions and his well-known adventurous approach won him many allies. I knew him well when I was still in charge at Aberdeen and respected his footballing methods. I knew his players very well, too, because they were among the best in Britain. And that's what baffled me about the United of the eighties. They had that giant Gordon McQueen at the back, an emerging Paul McGrath, and two very useful full backs in Arthur Albiston and Mike Duxbury. Then there was that mighty midfield - now that was something else. Steve Coppell, Arnie Muhren, Bryan Robson, Norman Whiteside, Remi Moses, Gordon Strachan. It always baffled me why they never won the League with that little lot. But, then, that's another story.

The fact is that after I replaced Ron, another generation of footballers had to sweep into my theatre of dreams before the greatest success of my life came true. I can now determine my own destiny as we roll towards the next century. But that position of control doesn't make me complacent. Far from it. I'm driven by an inner fear - a fear of failure.

The partying is over until this season's task in defending our precious title is fulfilled. You can rest assured it won't be surrendered without one hell of a fight. Everyone within Old Trafford is fully aware of the depth of commitment and sacrifice that was needed to turn us into champions after 26 years. And the crusade wasn't just mapped out over the last triumphant season. It began on the day I arrived, November 6th, 1986.

*"The singular factor that drives us Scots
is fear of failure and a compelling
determination to succeed. We cross the
border into England to prove ourselves."*

CHAPTER TWO

The Learning Curve

Fear was in my heart, deliberately well hidden but still gnawing at me deep down, on the first morning I walked into the Cliff training headquarters. It was a fear we have all endured at some time or other in our lives. The fear that some people can never quite conquer - the fear of the unknown.

When the chairman Martin Edwards offered me the United job, as big as any in the football world, I didn't hesitate. I wasn't afraid of being the man in charge at Old Trafford. Not at all. But there was a fear about crossing the border and coming down to work in England. It was the equivalent of stepping into another world. And when I arrived on the doorstep that November morning it forcibly hit me. All kinds of thoughts were racing through my mind. I didn't know anything about this great club, really. Didn't have a clue what the team was going to be. Didn't even know the make-up of the side in the Southampton Cup defeat that had brought Ron Atkinson the sack 48 hours earlier.

It wasn't quite panic stations, but I might well have sought diplomatic immunity at that particular moment if it had been on offer. Instead I had to square up to the players as they were summoned *en bloc* to the gym. True enough, no question at all, I was nervous. There was bound to be some resistance; they had, almost to a man, liked the big feller who had just bitten the bullet. I spoke to them on that issue, about the sense of loyalty and sadness at somebody losing a job, but there was also a message of determination from me that I wasn't going to be let down on certain counts. I might have been the come-lately management stranger to the majority of them, but they owed United, not any individual, their pride of performance. They had their own playing responsibilities and they must not be betrayed.

Next day, my United debut at Oxford, I watched, studied and then opened my mouth rashly when I would have been wiser to keep it shut. I confessed to the press gathering that the fitness of United's players was poor. I added that the problem would be resolved, and fast. But it was a mistake, because footballers, naturally enough overloaded with personal worries about working for a new boss, can become tense and tired when they suspect they are the target of a few early pot-shots. But during the next few weeks I detected deeper, even more alarming truths about the United team I had inherited. It wasn't equipped for the occasional rough-house rigours and combative nature of the League game at that time. They were always, I figured, going to be badly mashed and mauled at places like Wimbledon or Southampton. It wasn't a move towards revolution, but it was definitely a time for a major change. At that precise moment, when I reached my initial assessment of United's first team strength, the long campaign to be last season's champions actually began. It proved a long road to glory, admittedly, but it was a short conversation with the chairman, some time in the first weeks of 1987, that started it.

Searching for the new breed

As early as that first midwinter in the job I just couldn't see a successful future emerging from the existing players at United. Team selection was inconsistent because of individuals' being cursed by a record of injuries. Worse, there were no young, thrusting candidates jockeying for position. A new breed between, say, 19 and 23. And, just as worrying, we weren't really tough enough; when pitted against certain opposition we were simply unable to compete. The chairman was a little surprised when I broached the subject.

"You know, Martin," I said to him, "we need *seven* new players to sort it out." I suspect he hadn't reckoned on such a radical change. But he was sympathetic and chipped in with a number of concerns he had about the playing resources. Trouble was, so much transfer investment had already been made that there was very little spare gold bullion left in the United vault when I decided I needed to start spending.

But if the cash was missing, the evidence underpinning my footballing judgement never was. Ron's team could be very entertaining, no problem. They played with great style and verve. Outstanding displays of ability would have you on the edge of your seat and then, inexplicably, they would do something silly or careless in the final minute and career into a calamitous 2-1 defeat. I recall going to Anfield with them and beating Liverpool 1-0. Next day it was Norwich at Old Trafford in front of 53,000. We lost. Absolute madness. They could beat the best and lose to the worst. That had been United's tragic problem for twenty years or more. They have always been driven by their tradition to be the supreme adventurers; always having a go and yet not always caring about a little thing called defending.

I had players like Peter Barnes, for instance, who was really no use to me at all. I just couldn't see how he might contrive to produce a real threat. He had this great name and reputation, but I couldn't honestly appraise him as a top footballer. For sure he wasn't a good team player. Sometimes individuals, unluckily for them, are manœuvred around the game. They have too many moves. I believe Peter fell into that category. I'm afraid he had lost any sense of his own game, left mixed up from falling under the influence of too many guiding hands. His confusion inevitably meant he didn't produce enough and get what he might have done from football.

Jesper Olsen was another lightweight player of that United era, but I was far happier with his contribution. He had a natural enthusiasm in training work-outs and was always extremely receptive to advice. But he had one major flaw - a tendency to act casual at crucial moments when he had the team's fate resting at his boots. So often he would beat a defender or two, hit the by-line and then, through sheer carelessness, slice the cross out of bounds. Maddening for his team-mates who had bust a gut to make the box.

But, more than anything else, we just could not cope with both Jesper and Gordon Strachan in the same side. When we turned up at places like Wimbledon we ended up being completely mashed. Soccer's militant tendency were taking charge about that time. If you couldn't beat them, the option was to join them. To some degree anyway. It was a game of survival. Little Strach was okay because he was equipped with a mental toughness. But you couldn't succeed with too many of his ilk in one team. They weren't physically built to handle the popular football strategy in England at that time. It revolved heavily around the basics. Muscular set-pieces, the howitzer throw-in and the high ball bombardment employed by certain teams turned a game into Mission Impossible for the skillful but slimline players. And that's maybe another fundamental reason why United didn't win any titles.

Even Liverpool were forced to adapt when they faced the whack-'em Wombles. They won more prizes than any side in history with their pass-and-move approach. At Wimbledon, they abandoned the system. Out came a sweeper with Ian Rush and John Barnes down the middle to hold the ball when the rest could clear the defensive lines.

So I was not the only manager to see the necessity of reshaping my team's philosophy during that era.

However, it must be conceded, even now with the champions' prize resting in our grateful hands for at least a season, that if we had been granted Norman Whiteside's presence in the United team for a season or two longer the title could have been ours much sooner. Not just because he could play the heavy. Simply because he was some player.

Just the other day I reached for a video. It was big Norman playing in Ron's

Stormin' Norman

team when they destroyed West Brom 5-0 at the Hawthorns. It was another victory in the famous run of ten and, to be fair, might have been where that championship charge was seriously damaged. Remember Strach busting his collar bone as the fourth goal flew in the net? He was a real influence then. But Whiteside was quite simply unbelievable. An incredible footballer. They always told you he was slow but, let me tell you, he had a brain that was lightning. And, yes, ruthless as well. If I had been blessed with a young, fit and ambitious Norman, I genuinely believe we might not have been kept waiting until 1993 for the trophy we wanted most.

His career was a tragedy, for both player and club. That knee injury didn't just finish him at Everton; it killed him long before at United. If he had been blessed

Norman Whiteside - "quite simply unbelievable, an incredible footballer"

with better fitness, the likeable Irishman would have had a much brighter outlook on the football aspect of his life. I'm certain he would have ignored other distractions and concentrated more on the job, not walked on the wild side as much. But Norman suffered bouts of despair. He was gripped with it at times. It was easy enough to explain. Since the age of no more than 20, he had known he would be out of the business by 26 or 27. His long-standing knee damage was to blame and, unlike most players, you couldn't possibly kid him about it. Norman was keenly interested in physiotherapy and knew exactly what was happening to him in that treatment room.

He knew the score on the field as well. Norman was a shrewd operator. I'll never forget how he convinced me to sign Viv Anderson, a defender, to provide us with some steel, by provoking him to the point of clench-fisted retaliation in that infamous brawl with Arsenal. For sure, big Norm set that one up, and Viv fell for it hook line and sinker. But the way Viv behaved that day, showing he was a footballer prepared to stand up and be counted, convinced me more than anything I had to buy him.

They were scrapping in the tunnel before it was all over, but Whiteside called seconds out much earlier than that. In the first ten minutes he must have made a tackle on every man in the Arsenal team. Believe me, they didn't turn the other cheek. They tried to kick lumps out of him, but he just wouldn't get involved. Cute, he was. So cool and calculating about it. He was booked in the 23rd minute but never had one foul against him from that moment. Arsenal were frantic. Poor old David Rocastle got the red card, an Arsenal team-mate was booked for putting the boot in on Norman, and they were almost slavering for revenge. Norman set the time bomb ticking and then just stood back laughing at everybody else. He revelled in it while most of the rest were in a rage.

And that's when I decided I must have Anderson in my back four. He showed he had the bottle to play, flying into our box, throwing his head in where it can really hurt, and never looked for a corner to hide in when it all got a bit nasty. You could see he was a winner. I said quietly to myself he was a signing we had to make. And we worked on the subject for the rest of the season. In the summer he signed.

Norman, as so typically happens in the football brotherhood, became a very close ally of Viv once he arrived at United. Bosom pals you might say. But on the day of the brawl, it was a real eyeball job between the pair of them. Out on the pitch it had been an almost handbags-at-the-ready kind of confrontation. In the tunnel was the scene of the real action. Anderson was ready to fight everybody in sight. As George Graham reminded me recently, he had been really looking forward to our meeting for the first time and shaking my hand. Instead, look what happened. He almost ended up grabbing me by the throat before we even had time to say hello! It was chaos. Apart from Norman and Viv, David O'Leary and big Niall Quinn were intent on putting in their two pennyworth. Also keeping a watching brief was George's former coach Theo Foley and our own 'minder' Archie Knox, my now departed No. 2. And Archie, believe me, could cause a row in an empty house. So we had four Scots, four Irish and an Englishman squaring up. Enough to start another world war.

All about the survival instinct, really. It's in my own nature to be combative and that's why I appreciate the breed of player never likely to run for the shelters when certain situations develop. Like Viv Anderson, for example. A big, quick, resilient, influential full back. Trouble was that they never really accepted him on our terraces. And then the terrible curse of the Cliff casualty room claimed him as well. He had missed four games in almost four years for Arsenal. All through suspension. At our place he was constantly laid up with heel, knee and hip problems. They prevented him making a memorable impact at United.

Wanting the ball

But, for all my faith in Viv and football warriors of his kind, I have never employed a kicking team, the sort full of scowling intimidators, at any stage in my management career. Look at modern-day United. There's not a soul in that line-up that could really sort out a rival on the pitch. Not one. Sparky Hughes is, of course, a hard lad but he never hurts anybody. Never even thinks of inflicting serious damage no matter how much he is kicked. He's all blood and thunder, kids you on a bit, but there's no malice at all in that man. But he has always been extremely valuable to me and it was that competitive streak in him that made me pursue the return of Hughes virtually from my first weeks in the job.

I sensed there was terrace discord about him going to Barcelona, anyway, and he found it difficult to cope in Spain. When players of his age, around the 22 mark, are tempted abroad just for the money, it rarely works out. In Mark's case I was well aware it hadn't. He was too young and was without the bedrock of his marriage. Furthermore, at that time he was a a very quiet, introverted sort of character. Off the field, at least.

Once he tied the boots on, Sparky came to life. I love his type. Players who don't kow-tow to anybody. Not intimidated by threatening words or menacing actions. For me they fulfil the criterion for any footballer I was ever going to hand a wage packet to at United: they must have the bottle to perform at Old Trafford. Some can't. Very good players they might be, too. But with certain individuals the stage looms too large in their minds and destroys their ability to perform. I genuinely feel sorry for them. Little Terry Gibson was a classic case. He came to me one day and said the United scene, the great expectations and fierce demands of the place, were all a bit too much for him. He just couldn't cope with it. I must say there have been plenty more like him.

Mark Hughes - "The first principle of success at United is that you must want the ball."

The first principle of being a success at United is that you must want the ball. No matter what you are going to do with it that desire has got to be there. If it isn't, if any player is simply running scared of having the ball, he is doomed. He might as well walk out of the building, and not waste any more time. Ours or his. I have applied that code in making certain not a single player on the staff is going to crack mentally under the pressure. They all have plenty of guts. I underline it with a very plain request.

"Just look around this dressing-room," I tell the first team lads. "Make sure you take a close look at every single individual and you should all be saying, 'I'm glad I have got him on my side.' If you can't then we have a problem." But these days I don't believe we have. If there is a war, in the football sense that is, we know we have the right men in the trenches. Every one of them is solid. It's a team that won't give in. They don't have to behave like thugs to prove they are hard nuts to crack. Consider Brian McClair. He has got such depths of mental strength, on and off the field. He came down from Celtic, across the border into a football environment he couldn't be expected to know, and he knocked in 32 goals in his first season. No one since George Best had managed that at this club. That's what I call being a toughie. No matter who is on his back, crowd or opponent, he always wants the ball. That's the secret.

I can also put forward my old sparring partner Strachan as another example. He's only a diminutive guy, but what character. A strong man of a different kind. For two years when I was in charge at Aberdeen he was absolutely sensational. I must admit I never saw that level of performance from Gordon in our time together at United. Fleeting moments, yes, great moments occasionally, but never the level of consistency that I expected. Read that as an objective criticism, but certainly not a condemnation. Because good game or bad, the bottom line was always that he desperately wanted the ball. Exactly the mental courage I appreciate. In fact, I demand it.

I want he-man heroes, no matter what shape or size, not fancy wimps in my United teams. It's been the method I have applied in measuring the true worth of all my players since the day I arrived. But I will not accept the charge levelled at me in certain quarters that I started off here as a defensively minded manager. That I was an exponent of self-protectionist football. They even said I brought it down with me from Scotland. Not true. That has never been part of my football culture. My team talks have always centred on going forward - as a team, mind. Not reckless but always going forward. My way of doing things might have been different to Big Ron's - obviously no manager is the same - but it has always been a positive strategy.

Just ask Willie Miller and Alex McLeish at Aberdeen. Or Steve Bruce and Gary Pallister, for that matter. Down the years all four of them have complained to me about their back four responsibilities. They definitely wouldn't agree that my tactical plans are shaped around a barricade of defenders. My centre-backs are always expected to play in a one-on-one pattern with the full backs pushed forward of them. If they are efficient at their jobs, they should be able to read the game and adjust. But I do accept that I base a great deal of tactical importance on having the right men in the middle at the back. It was an issue I was determined to deal with as soon as I arrived. Too many of the candidates for those two important positions could claim Casualty as their middle name. Kevin Moran, a terrific competitor, gave you his heart and soul every time he played. But at that time he was a treatment room regular. McGrath, too. He always seemed to be injured. Graeme Hogg and Billy Garton the same. At times I had to use the adaptable Mike Duxbury, even Frank Stapleton, in there. He never let me down. But it was an unsatisfactory situation, forever having to juggle with a department of the team I saw as crucial.

In that area I insisted on consistency, both in performance and identity of the performers. I demanded an effective axis like Miller and McLeish at Aberdeen. Miller, for instance, was fantastic. If there is one lingering regret about my years in management it is that I didn't have wonderman Willie and runaround Robbo together in a team of mine. In the competitive sense they are like twins. If you ever see a photograph of them it's uncanny. There is a sort of glazed look about their eyes. It reveals a fierceness and incredible concentration that they both possess.

For all McGrath's outstanding, inborn qualities, I never saw that in him. His potential was enormous. But he would go to sleep at the back sometimes and that bothered me. I needed a quick cure. I had to have defensive discipline. It didn't take too much ferreting around other football clubs for me to determine the man who was made to measure. Steve Bruce was the name. And he has proved he was worth every single penny of the investment. In more than five years he has not missed more than half a dozen matches for us. Since Gary Pallister's arrival alongside Brucie, they have been the bedrock of the team. And, I might add, the championship as well. If you analysed Steve's game you might not finish up with too flattering a synopsis for a top level centre-back. Think about it. He's not quite six foot; closer to twelve stone than the ideal thirteen; not quick at all, in fact maybe a bit on the slow side; his left foot is a little bit dodgy too. So why the hell buy him, you might ask. Hand that breakdown to a manager in the transfer market and he would probably sling it in the bin. But this is a classic case where all the parts don't make the whole.

Because Bruce has got something you can't truly define in a fact file. He's blessed with a heart as big as a house; the complete competitor. And sometimes in a footballer that can be everything. Some people shape their lives, make fantastic careers, out of the basic asset of overwhelming, almost bottomless enthusiasm to be a success. Bruce is certainly one who falls perfectly into that mould. He cost me less than a million, but in so many ways he has been our priceless investment.

For supporters that kind of whole-hearted endeavour and bravado for the cause allows them to close their eyes and forgive any other failing. Count me in, too. Fans across the whole country are being asked a sizeable slice of their weekly wage packets to follow their favourite teams. In return they rightly deserve more than anything a team that really tries for them. You might be down the pan three-nil, but the desire, urgency and energy must still be committed to the cause every second of the way to that last blast of the whistle.

Their reward, even in defeat, is, for instance, the spectacle of good old Sparky flying in among the boots or hurling himself at startled defenders to close them down; Incey and Pop going hell for leather in the middle of the park; Brucie on one of his *kamikaze* charges. And, just occasionally, Peter Schmeichel quitting his goalmouth, as he did against Villa, to try and score himself at a late set piece. For a moment it strikes you with horror: has he gone raving mad or something? But then you realise. They have huge, great, fighting hearts and they just don't want to be beaten. My teams, I insist, have that quality, no matter whatever else other people might claim they lack.

Fergie's Fledglings

Crowds can tell you so much about the real heartbeat of the game. I reflect back on a crunch period for me midway through the '88/'89 season. By that stage I realised I had to get my act together and have a go. The terraces, too, were beginning to murmur with impatience. The problem for me was that I didn't have the depth of resources to do much at all. So many of the significant performers at the club were again being plagued by injury troubles. So I turned to the kids. They became known, nation-wide, as the Fergie Fledglings. The name was nice and neat, but not quite accurate. They weren't really my players. I had inherited them, except for Lee Sharpe. But they did a magnificent job all the same, buying

Lee Sharpe - a fledgling high-flier.

time for the restructuring that carried us to eventual success last season. I knew, though, that most of them weren't top drawer material. Not footballers who would survive at United and forge lasting reputations. Sharpey, of course, was guaranteed a future, even then. Lee Martin is also an excellent player and one other, Tony Gill, would have made a good pro if his career hadn't been wrecked by injury. The clinical judgement on the rookies wasn't so important, though. They were what the crowd wanted in that period of United's evolution - and they responded to them with a real, unbridled fervour.

It told me everything about this club. A brief lesson that arguably compared with a decade of learning. I've always said that when a football club drafts a contract for an incoming manager, it should contain a clause guaranteeing five years' experience as well as all the other bits and pieces. Because until you have completed that kind of period - the learning curve - you just don't know what it's all about. But it didn't take anything like that long for me to absorb the weekly lessons of the English game. At its core, even more so three or four years ago, it had a very strong physical content.

The strategy of most teams meant play was carried through on the basis of aerial and physical combat. Everton, for example, were champions twice in the eighties with a powerful team of aggressive, athletic players. They employed plenty of the long ball approach and quickly banished any notion that Goodison Park was the soccer academy that once made it famous. Even then, I accept Liverpool stuck to the traditional values of a pass-and-move team, but they were still galvanised by the likes of Steve McMahon, Steve Nichol and, before he left for Italy, their current manager, Graeme Souness. You wouldn't describe any of them exactly as shy, retiring types.

So when, in my early United days, I reached that crucial assessment of what needed to change, the management manual on how to succeed didn't need to be overblown or complex. Get tougher or go under was roughly the code we had to obey. Instantly, I knew I had personally to handle United's daily training work-outs. Fitness levels needed to be improved rapidly. Two or three of the senior players were in pretty poor shape and fitness grades generally were considerably below what they should have been. I made certain, even if pockets of resistance showed at the start, that a hard graft regime in the week would provide us with obvious benefits on Saturday afternoon. The whole place had become a little slack.

Get tough or go under

The lifestyle of the players had to be quickly addressed and improved. It's a topic I have referred to before and it's no secret what I felt about standards of behaviour. But reading Arnie Muhren's book certainly opened my eyes to problems that inevitably meant the team's competitive edge was going to be blunted. The book proved I wasn't the only person who thought certain aspects on the playing side were far from being right. A lot of the lads were enjoying themselves during the day, and away from the football environment, more than they should have been. You could pick up the daily gossip about it all over Manchester. The cynics joked about United being more of a social club than a football club. No longer. That sort of nonsense is very much history these days.

So are quite a few of the important players of that era. They had to depart because too many were around the thirty mark. I had a fair few with well-established international reputations, earned with distinction in their time. But their time had gone. I couldn't see myself creating any sort of championship future with their surviving in my team. They had to go. Any kind of hesitation might have been fatal - for me.

And the singular factor that drives us Scots more than anything else is the fear of failure. Or, perhaps, it should more correctly be recognised as a fear of failure and a compelling determination to succeed. All of us, myself as much as anybody in history, crossed the border into England to prove ourselves. I suppose it might all be wrapped up in the invader syndrome and the history of conflict between our rival countries down the years. We are here and we exist to be winners. I recall the great period in the sixties and seventies when there was literally a mass invasion of Scottish schoolboys into the English game. They swamped the place. Peter Lorimer, Billy Bremner, Eddie Gray and Bobby Moncur were all filled with that huge tartan desire to be the best, and not carry the brand of failure. So, too, a little later did Joe Jordan and

With fellow Scot George Graham - "we are here and we exist to be winners"

Gordon McQueen. The route had been well plotted, decades before they even got a mention, by the likes of Sir Matt Busby and Bill Shankly. Nowadays the generation of Scots who can't stop winning takes in George Graham, Kenny Dalglish and Graeme Souness.

They are all fired and motivated by the basic instinct of conquering life and finishing top of the pile. The fear of failure, if you make it of course, is quickly swept aside and replaced by great public expectations. And that demand can be just as challenging. But, at last, I do now feel in control of this massive football club, and in command of my own sporting destiny. Once, not very long ago either, I might not honestly have dared make that statement.

As they say in Lancashire, I'm feeling just champion after all.

*"For the first time since the day
I arrived, United's crowd turned against
me. I went home feeling very low and
just locked the door on everybody."*

CHAPTER THREE

Black December

There have been times of deep despair, as well as days of rich rewards at Old Trafford. The mere reminder of what I call my own Black December, in 1989, still makes me shudder.

It was, without question, the lowest, most desperate point ever in all my years in management. For a while I became something of a soccer recluse, driven into a self-imposed hiding by the failure I hate. I shut the world outside my door and just felt miserable.

To be honest, we weren't playing too badly at the time. But in front of goal we couldn't burst a paper bag. We just couldn't knock the ball in the net often enough. It left us with a pretty grim performance record, with a run of eight games delivering six defeats and two draws. The darkest period I have ever suffered in the game. Next match we faced the awkward squad from Crystal Palace and I gambled. I dropped Mark Hughes and opted for sending young Mark Robins, a natural predator, up the park with Choccy McClair. The day was pure misery. It was coming down in buckets and I wondered if somebody up

there really didn't like me. But we came out of the blocks well, started impressively and life-saver McClair scored early. Then, with seconds to go to half time, Mark Bright poached an equaliser. A bit of a blow, but we could survive. He wasn't finished at that, though, and a minute after we came back out he had the ball in the net again. Palace in front 2-1. Suddenly, I felt like a fugitive with the eyes of a very hostile world focused on me. For the first time since the day I had arrived three years before, United's crowd turned against me. I went home feeling very low and just locked the door on everybody. Looking back, I suppose for a while I turned into something of a hermit. I couldn't face people; I wouldn't go out anywhere.

At that time, I felt like some sort of a traitor to the United support. I stayed indoors. Never strayed from the house unless it was to carry out my daily duties with the players and at the club. Archie Knox tried his best to bring me out of a mood of sheer despondency and gloom.

"This is silly," he would say, "You can't lock yourself away for life. Let's go out together." But I wouldn't budge. I was adamant. Until I was a winner I wouldn't be seeing too many outsiders. None probably. The whole situation was deeply, seriously, affecting my life for a short period. I believe most people who know me would accept that I am a fairly strong character and that I wouldn't allow my personal frustration to cross the borders of my job responsibilities. For instance, I didn't let it influence my decisions when picking the team, no matter what the outside pressures. My despondency never crept into my other United duties and I always showed my positive side, never betraying any fear or anxiety to the players. Or to the press.

Deliberately, I made certain I was buoyant and upbeat about the situation when talking to reporters. They had to get the right message across from me. It was very much a conscious effort on my part. I made certain I could never be portrayed as the merchant of doom: my verdict was meant to be confident and optimistic. I was always meticulously well prepared on what I intended to say. I made sure of that. The last thing I needed was for me, the manager of United, to be seen as a blabbering fool. When people are weak they often say misguided things and then it's easy to suggest they have blown it completely. I wasn't going to be that sucker.

But after the Palace defeat, I don't mind admitting, I found it almost impossibly hard to handle what was happening. So that night when the FA Cup draw was being made I was slumped at home in front of the box trying to figure out the future. Then the phone rang. It was a journalist wanting my reaction to the team we had pulled in the Cup. It was the ultimate nightmare... Forest, at that time very much Wembley specialists and the team that had sent us crashing in the quarter-final the year before. What did I think? "Pass me the rope" is what I thought. For a moment I really started to believe I had been cursed. Think about it. I had just been beaten 2-1 at home by Stevie Coppell's Palace, the crowd had virtually howled me out of the ground and I had dropped Sparky, their big hero. And, after all that, I had pulled Cloughie's lot out of the hat who, in that period, were the best Cup team in the country. Of course, I told the journalist in

*Under a
cloud*

question, I was feeling absolutely wonderful about it all!

Even with time to prepare, nobody gave us a prayer against Forest. They were, I'm sure, pretty certain it was going to be a hanging job for me. Fair enough, I have never been in a worse managerial position than when approaching that away tie, and I have probably never felt more cornered by a situation in my life. But you can never visualise getting the sack. It's never going to happen to you, so you think, and it's automatically wiped from the mind as a threat. You appreciate, of course, that it happens. Always to other people, though, that's the subconscious message. Never to you. And you don't know how the sacking is served up. Whether the chairman makes a phone call, writes you a letter or you read about it in the newspaper next morning. Whatever, it was never much of an issue in my mind even in those desperately troubled times. Privately, though, I did think: "You have to get your act together now, Fergie. You have to get your finger out, or it *is* going to happen to you."

The players were under strict orders as well. I told them as the team bus pulled into Cloughie's territory, the front forecourt at Forest, that they must all wear a huge smile to make sure we destroyed the gallows mentality being created around our Cup tie. You learn very rapidly at United that it's important at times to put on a front. And never was it more important than that particular day in our history, in our progress towards being champions of England. The zoom lenses of the press pack were all trained intently on us as we clambered off the bus. Let's not mess about with fancy language: they were there for my burial, weren't they? I can still remember very vividly the comments of TV pundit Jimmy Hill before a ball was kicked. He said we looked a beaten team - and that was only in the warm-up! It's the sort of reaction you expect from modern day television coverage and general media hysteria. But coming from somebody like Hill, a man with a football background, it was a little surprising, to say the least.

Votes of confidence

I just had to swallow hard and accept it as part of all the mischief and sensationalism centred on United at the time. Hill was just adding fuel to the supposed funeral pyre and all the hype that threatened: "If Fergie loses this one, then he's out." I knew differently, of course. My chairman had spoken to me a couple of days previously and promised, win or lose at Forest, I was safe from the sack. Which was reassuring, considering he was under press bombardment to give me a public vote of confidence. Martin rightly indicated that if he did that it would be my death knell. Quietly, he told me he would not, in any case, insult me with such a manœuvre.

I fully appreciate I had really to climb out of a very deep pit, and one that appeared to be deepening almost daily at that time. But it's amazing, on reflection, how small factors play an important part in your life when everything seems so grim and forbidding. I'll never forget, for instance, the two heart-lifting letters that dropped on my doorstep in the build-up to the big game.

One was from my first-ever chairman at East Stirling. He himself was a man of great presence and determination. His letter, I recall, went something along the lines of: "You show 'em, son. Is this the same Alex Ferguson that I knew as a young lad, that I presented with his first chance in management? The one that I saw running full-pelt down the track towards a linesman in a rage, the one I had to haul back from any trouble? Is this the same man who is going to give in easy now at Manchester United?" When I read it, that letter really sat me up in my chair and made me think. A day or two later a second letter arrived. It was from an old school teacher and it contained a replica of the first football medal I ever won. I collected mine playing in his team and it was his medal, wrapped in a well-penned message that read: "This is just to remind you of what you have achieved so far in life and what your father did for you. So don't buckle now, and don't ever surrender. Remember what you are made of and that's more than merely the make-up of a football manager."

He was underlining, I suspected, the very significant point that, however threatened you feel, you should never forget the ability that got you where you are in the first place. When you have been pummelled by a few alarming set-backs, the natural reaction is to forget that. Instead, the overwhelming worry that descends on you like an avalanche is what the hell you have to do to get yourself out of the hole. Sometimes you don't have to do anything at all. Most times, in fact, you simply have to be yourself. If you are blessed with perseverance and unflinching determination, that's all you need. Plus the self-belief to carry it through. Don't ever be demoralised, crushed, by a few defeats on a football field. It was another lesson in life. So thanks, gentlemen, because those two letters helped to steady my perspective on what might have developed into a full-blown crisis.

Reinforced, off we went in search of Cloughie's scalp. Never easy at the best of times, but this felt more like the worst of times and my selection options were as seriously undermined as my confidence. If you asked the most committed United die-hard what my side was that day, I reckon nine out of ten would get it wrong. Out were Robson, Ince, Sharpey, Danny Wallace, Mal Donaghy, Colin Gibson and Neil Webb. We certainly had something of a job on that afternoon.

Enough is enough

But I felt relaxed, I was positive, and I led an advance party down to the Forest ground first thing in the morning. I needed to check everything, make sure each element of my preparation was perfect. So much had to be right that day and I knew it. I roamed the pitch, marking out the width, going over every inch. The rough bits, the soft patches. Painstaking stuff. In pressure situations like that you look for the nearest relief valve, but the only moments of relaxation spared me were on the bus. Joined by our assistant secretary Ken Ramsden and the kit manager Norman Davies, we indulged in a daft game of cards. Knockout whist at a grand a game! You know, I still haven't collected on my £60,000 winnings to this day. I have to admit I'm not too concerned - there was an even more precious prize to be seized that day.

I knew my build-up had been good. No problems with the team briefing either. Confident, assertive, upfront. It had to be, with so much at stake. In my bones I sensed before kick-off that the players were going to fight like hell. Oh yes, we were in a crusading mood. And any team fighting a cause amounts to the most dangerous and menacing in football. In that situation all you need is one move, a spark that ignites the team into a roaring inferno. We got it.

It lives with me even now. Little Russell Beardsmore worked a neat one-two down the left flank with Lee Martin and peeled back the Forest cover right away. The ball was turned back into the box for Mark Robins to hold it up. Flying in alongside him was McClair, literally begging for a simple touch. One roll from Robins and Choccy would have been unloading a shot. Instead Robins turned and took a pop himself. The 'keeper flung himself and the chance was gone, spinning wide of a post from a very good save. But that was our first attack and I knew it would trigger the impetus of the whole team. There was, all of a sudden, a good smell about the place for us.

So it was sweet when the goal rippled the Forest netting. If you've lost the detail over the passage of time, let me fill you in. It was inspired, I promise, by an absolutely magnificent tackle by full back Martin, who was to be an even bigger hero in winning us the Cup itself a few months later. There is something that rouses the fans about one of those thunderous, pile-driver tackles when a player emerges with the ball at his feet. Drives the terraces wild. This was one such occasion. Lee ambushed Gary Crosby, in possession close to the half-way line, and threaded it in to Mark Hughes. Outside of the boot, cool as you like, and Sparky clipped it swiftly and accurately into the Forest box.

Now for a bit of controversy. Stuart Pearce, desperate to clamp down on the danger, actually fouled Robins, shoving him in the back as he made the angled run. There was bedlam on the bench, we were all screaming ourselves silly: "Ref, for God's sake, that's a penalty!" But the push did, in fact, help Robins. He normally would have tried to flick it in the corner. Instead, because of Mr. Pearce's little 'assist', he was falling slightly and stuck his header away in the opposite direction.

"Never mind the effing penalty, ref, that's a damn good goal!" we all bellowed. It was a quicker change of mind than ever occurred to any politician. So the little hit man, who eventually became impatient and moved on to Norwich, had saved us. For him there must always be a special mention in the fairytale.

But I know who really won us that match - our fans. The support was simply defiant. At least ten thousand of them that day, and a bloody-minded bunch. They were not going to surrender, no way. Each time we won a throw-in they were off their seats; they roared every time we came through a tackle; and a shot at goal was the nearest thing to a civic reception! They helped to create the cause, that stirring of patriotic blood, that I mentioned earlier. It always works. Because they were down didn't mean they were going to be shoved further into the gutter. They rose to the challenge, just like the players.

Me? I relied, like so many football managers of past generations, on a little superstition. For often unfathomable reasons it just seems to crop up and play a role in sporting success. In my case it was a cricket-style sweater in the United colours that I bought in that bleak midwinter from the souvenir shop. I wore it first on the morning of the Forest tie. And I dragged on that sweaty old jumper, along with the same set of clothing, all the way to Wembley that season. Every Friday night and every Saturday as well. By the end the players were giving me some terrible stick, holding their noses and telling me they couldn't wait to win the Cup. Just so I would get rid of the jumper. But it stayed on my back until we had seen off Palace in the Final replay.

Teamwork...

Leading by example

Just another day at the office

Denis tells new boy Roy "lean on me"

Paul and Lee share a joke on the sidelines

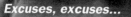
Excuses, excuses...

Pally, Fergie, Robbo and Brucie

Ryan and Lee get on down

Bryan Robson - "a legend to rest comfortably alongside the likes of Bobby Charlton and George Best"

Eric Cantona - "my greatest wish is that he enjoys life at United more than anywhere else"

Mark Hughes - "his competitive streak makes him a must for United"

"If I could be remembered for anything when I finish in management, it wouldn't be for all the Cups, the titles and glory. It would be for one thing - that I never deserted any one of the players I have had under my control."

CHAPTER FOUR

Planning for the Future

Granted the benefit of hindsight, I might have been better snapping up my good luck charm a year earlier. Before we met Forest in the FA Cup quarter final - and lost. Because if Eric Cantona is rightly acclaimed as the catalyst in our title success last season, that disaster with Forest was the specific date when I was galvanised into the broadly based action that effectively made United a club side worthy of being champions. It was, hands on heart, my moment of truth.

In the aftermath of what I considered a terrible defeat, I made my mind up - enough is enough. That was my point of exhaustion. Aye, without a shadow of doubt, that was when I lost my tether with the old team and decided in effect that Manchester just wasn't big enough for the both of us. Somebody had to go - and it wasn't going to be me. I wasn't to be the sacrifice.

That beating from Clough's team was worse, I think, than any other. Not because of the size of the defeat but because of what it meant. The implications of it all. Honestly, I just thought to myself: "This is really not worth it. I am not going through this agony anymore. I am not going to have myself finishing second to Liverpool for another season. No, definitely, I'm not going to have it." I had reached a stage where I just couldn't tolerate that level of team performance. Whatever happened, I was simply not going to suffer and take it anymore.

I confided in the chairman. Without taking up too much of his time I insisted that drastic action was necessary to drag the club round. It was my second full season and the revolution had to rumble. That week I sold Strach to Leeds. We lost at the weekend and little Gordon was gone by Wednesday. I just felt I had built him up to get us to Wembley that season. We had done well, admittedly, but I was so desperately disappointed when we lost in the last eight. There were no ifs or buts then. Just one radical conclusion: I had to build a brand-new team.

At the next board meeting I marched in with my detailed plan for United's future. The directors listened carefully as I explained the pruning I was prepared to make. Strach had already gone, of course, so that money was in the transfer kitty already. I assured them it would be shortly increased by the departures of Norman Whiteside and Paul McGrath. Heroes they might be, but they had to be traded for the buy-in phase. I asked the board to support what was, admittedly, a major reconstruction. I emphasised that I had already released Peter Davenport, Chris Turner and Graeme Hogg. Colin Gibson would be on his way as well once we received a realistic offer for him. I urged the directors to believe me when I said that, basically, I could do no more. This was very serious surgery. I was sweeping aside virtually a whole team to lay down the long-term policies. In the process I accepted I was leaving myself exposed and pretty thin on the ground with a diminished first team squad.

The Shopping List

| Paul Ince | Neil Webb | Gary Pallister | Michael Phelan |

Next I revealed the names of the players I believed were necessary to inject United with a new urgency for future success. Five of the best, I figured. I spelled them out. Paul Ince and Stuart Pearce headed the list because they were both soon to be out of contract with their clubs. Gary Pallister and Neil Webb were also definite targets. Michael Phelan, because of his all-round options as a player, was also under serious consideration. Eventually, the only one I missed out on was Pearce. I had been working on him for a while. I thought I was going to land him, too, but experience taught me subsequently that Cloughie can kid you on a little in the buying market. The remainder eventually arrived, along with the addition of Danny Wallace from Southampton. That's when, I suppose, a different kind of problem needed to be resolved. First of all we had a newly-arrived bunch of recruits all landing in town within a matter of weeks. All booked into hotels until, sometimes for as long as six months, they could sell and buy property of their own. Little Danny, for instance, was holed up with his wife and children for ages in that kind of away-from-home environment. It definitely tells on players and affects their performances.

The other aspect, on the field rather than off it, is bedding down so many new players in the side together. Footballers are no different from anybody else moving to a new employer - they need time to settle in the job. That's exactly what happened with us. For a while the whole team didn't operate to the highest level of efficiency. And that maybe explains why we struggled in the League that season and blew it at Forest. But that's an explanation, not an indictment. I would never betray or belittle my playing staff by marking them down as individual scapegoats for our collective failure. Examples of it spring easily to mind. It's been going on in our game for years - get yourself off the hook by volunteering another victim. But you can reach some very telling judgements about people by watching closely how they react in a tight corner. Like the moral of the sinking ship when the rats dive off and make sure they are saved. That's not in my nature.

If I could be remembered for anything when I finish in management, it wouldn't be for all the Cups, the titles and glory I might have helped to secure. It would be for one thing - that I never turned in, deserted in other words, any one of the players I have had under my control down the years. I accept I am ruthless in picking my teams. My undisputed loyalty is to the club, not to any individual. My first responsibility is to be a winner for United and if people must suffer heartache as a consequence, that's just the rules of the game. But outside of that kind of discipline I am not ruthless at all. If one of my players is in trouble, I'll answer the call anywhere. It wouldn't matter if it were five in the morning. I would be on his doorstep right away. You have to earn their understanding and loyalty and in blaming, say, striker Joe Bloggs, for losing a match is a one-way ticket to disaster among any squad of players. Mine, the present crop of champions, never provoke too much alarm anyway. They are here to stay. When they were signed at a cost of several million it was always designed to be a long-term investment. If we didn't secure the title in the first year, I knew they would still be highly competitive as a unit for at least five years. They were really covered by a championship guarantee in allowing me several attempts at the top prize with the same solid base of players. The major mechanics had all been completed - now it was all down to a little tinkering and fine-tuning. They had been built to last.

The emergence of Paul Ince, for instance, in the last three years is really a mirror image of Manchester United's own improvement and development into

The making of Paul Ince

the title winners of '93. Through self-examination and critical scrutiny he has turned himself into a big-stage player and, every step of the way, he has been followed by a team that I believe is destined to make their own lasting impact on our national game. The championship was merely the kick-off, not the final whistle.

But it was *the* Final, the FA Cup replay victory over Palace, that effectively marked Incey's initial breakthrough as a footballer with both the ability and heroic qualities you need. One man can never make a team, but one match can make a player. And Wembley was the first indication of Paul's growing maturity and influence. If he hadn't completely broken down all the barriers, the welcoming gates of Old Trafford had certainly been given a fair old shove by our Cockney rebel. He was exactly that - a rebel - when he arrived. But there wasn't

Paul Ince - "a big-stage player"

much sign of the rebellious nature in the first game with Palace. He ended up, as I remember, as a chronic victim of cramp and was walking around the pitch like a twisted duck! For the last ten minutes I slotted him into the right full back role and he looked like he was playing on stilts. Comical to watch, but in the replay he showed his athletic stature and the skills of a player truly coming of age in front of a world audience.

The quality of his performance, as I reflect on it now, was an important brick in our championship foundation. The boy from London's East End has been a barometer for the United of the nineties. Chart his progress and you also chart the rebuilt team's climb to the top. Not long after he arrived I saddled him with what was meant as a compliment, and could have been a curse, in suggesting he was the new Robson. But to give my words of praise some credibility, I also emphasised that Paul must survive several important phases in

his career. First he was to establish himself with us; next prove he had the capabilities, responsibilities and leadership to be a captain of United and England; then demonstrate he was a footballer who could boss a side; and also become a potent goalscorer. Bit by bit, he has come through them all.

I am not arguing that he has always been entirely the axis of United's success, but his emergence and progress has been a point of importance in our development: he has been our renaissance factor if you like. Just about now, at the age of 25, he is reaching towards maturity. Maybe Paul has even surprised himself with his role reversal out on the park. He has clearly appreciated that he needs, in intense moments of competitive pressure, to keep his mouth shut and get rid of the chip on his shoulder. The fact that he managed to do all of that proved that he was able to identify a problem that threatened to restrict his whole future and could do something about it. Drastic measures were needed and, voluntarily, he opted for them. I can easily tune in to that psychological breakthrough. It was similar to my own experience when I arrived at United. I rapidly acknowledged that certain demands had to be laid down at the club, otherwise I would never be a champion. Incey has squared up to himself and said: "I have got to buckle down or I am never going to achieve what I want with my club and country." There has been a very private self-appraisal that has paid dividends in his public playing career. He is now moving rapidly in the direction of becoming a highly distinguished midfield player. Almost at the point of creating an aura for himself.

For so long we have been made to live in the shadow of legends. Players of the incredible stature of George Best, Bobby Charlton and Denis Law, for example, have loomed large over all of us. But now we have great players as well to match the most famous of United's earlier generations. Like Eric Cantona, Bryan Robson and, slowly but surely, Ince himself. They are the ones the emerging kids of today put on pedestals. They are taking over as the role models who fire youthful ambition. The heroes that you need at any club.

Right from the early days I never had any doubts that Ince would establish himself at Old Trafford. The only slight worry, naturally kept close to my chest at the time, was Paul's coming north from London harbouring maybe something of a suspicion of life in these parts. Swiftly, though, he leapt over that particular hurdle. Marriage was the crucial factor. It might sound like an old-fashioned position to adopt, but I like all my players to be married with a couple of toddlers around the home. You are guaranteed a consistent level of behaviour when a footballer has a stable family background. It puts him on an even path.

Now I am absolutely certain that Ince, having survived his growing-up period as a footballer, is going to be a United captain during my time as manager. He has already underlined his leadership qualities at the highest level. He is quite a giving, generous bloke when you get to know him. At first Incey might be a little circumspect, even suspicious, but once the bridge of trust is firmly in place you have a loyal pal for life. One classic example was his public stand on behalf of the England manager when the national team were in a state of siege and being hammered from all directions. Only days earlier, Graham Taylor had called his internationals a bunch of 'headless chickens' but that didn't stop Incey defending him when it mattered. That tells you something about his strength of character.

Painful decisions

When I signed Ince, in that huge sea change for the club in the late eighties, it was to send a message to the fans. I wanted to tell them we were still alive, not a spent force, that we had some substance. And I wanted to show exactly what I was made of. By the time we reached Wembley, though, I was delivering a very different message for one individual in particular. It didn't carry any hope, only heartbreak in fact, for Jim Leighton. He wasn't a Wembley scapegoat, but a sacrifice that had to be made, the head that had to roll to safeguard the whole future of a new team. Jim, understandably, took it badly. Very badly. When you lose a player's trust, confidence and respect, as happened in Jim's case, he ends up feeling very bitter and you lose him forever. I accept that by dropping my number one goalkeeper for the Palace replay I destroyed his future at United. That decision ended his career with us for sure. But I still maintain I did him a favour and, even if I had picked him to play, he was finished anyway. He had already lost the faith of the fans. There was no way back for him.

Uppermost in my mind was that United were in the Cup Final and they needed to win it. Correction, they *had to* win it. We just couldn't afford to submit to Palace, one of the less significant clubs in the Premier League at that time. Against, say, Liverpool or Arsenal you might be able to plead a case. I couldn't have raised an argument if Stevie Coppell's players had whipped us. It would have been unforgivable and would certainly have halted, if not destroyed, the impetus of our campaign to be back among the best. So Leighton had to go, there was just no happy solution for me to take. After the first game, I looked across at him in our dressing-room. He was a beaten man. His head was almost between

Jim Leighton - "took it like a knife to the heart"

his knees. Jim knew in his heart he had just had an absolute stinker. I could see he had cracked and was at his lowest point, his confidence shattered. Psychologically, he just wasn't in the right frame of mind to take on Palace again. If he had made one more mistake out on that pitch, it would have seriously damaged the whole team and I'm pretty certain we wouldn't have won the Cup. For the rest of that week Leighton was completely shell-shocked.

So the tough, cold-eyed decision had to be made by me. Physically and mentally Jim was wrecked as a goalkeeper for a game that could dictate the destiny of so many people. If team selection was a matter of loyalty or respect, Leighton would definitely have been in it because I had known him for most of my management life. But those couldn't be factors. It was a decision I had to base on sheer animal instinct because it had to be for the survival of Manchester United. There is no question about that. I had to forget who I was dealing with, isolate the manager's personal considerations, and remember just one thing - this club. Every other emotive issue was wiped from my mind. I had, remember, given Jim his first team debut for Aberdeen against Hearts at Tynecastle when he was just eighteen. I had brought him from Scotland to Old Trafford in the early days and he had been my goalkeeper for a long time, helping me towards a great deal of football success down the years. So it was a decision that inevitably tortured the mind. Archie Knox and myself debated the ramifications of the whole affair for ages the day before the replay. But when I approached the crunch, I don't think Archie expected it. For some reason he believed I would change my mind at the last moment. He would have left Jim in, I know that, for the sake of continuity and the fact that we had reached Wembley with him in the side. And even when I made the team announcement Archie hadn't realised Leighton was out.

When I pulled Jim to one side it was admittedly a terrible experience. He took it like a knife to the heart. When you leave a player out, no matter what you say or the compassion you attempt to get across, it's like being in an empty chamber. The words of explanation just seem to echo round and round. Jim wasn't really listening, he wasn't taking it in, because any player in his position doesn't agree with you anyway. It doesn't matter if you take the blame for the whole business and sympathise. The fall guy in that desperate situation is just not interested in the reasons why he won't be out there with his mates playing the big game.

It can be a very messy business indeed. I'm told that at Liverpool the first inkling the players have whether they have been dropped is when the sheet is pinned to the board. I can understand exactly why they do that because when you have an awkward issue to resolve with a player it can affect your own preparation. You can easily be plunged into a confrontation with an individual, so my own method is to handle everything decisively, quickly, and get it over with at least 30 minutes before the team briefing. Before players start muttering and whispering among themselves. But whatever approach you take it can never be easy. There have been other very delicate decisions during my time in management, but the Leighton affair inevitably grabbed headlines because he had spent so much of his career with me at both Aberdeen and United. In that position you just pray and hope you reach the right conclusion; you can't afford to be wrong. I still recall the important part of my heart-to-heart with Jim: "I could be wrong on this, but I'm convinced I'm right, and that's why I'm doing this and dropping you from the team. It's for the club, for the rest of the players, and for you as well."

I haven't spoken to Jim much since that day. We were involved in a few, shall we say, businesslike conversations when I was trying to get him another club. But it was very clear during those meetings that I had lost him. All I could do was resolve the predicament by finding him a club as rapidly as possible. Eventually, although I still regarded Jim as a very competent goalkeeper, I let him go to Dundee for virtually nothing.

Farewell to a supersub

Another headline-maker and major talking point of that successful Cup campaign has also subsequently quit the camp. Mark Robins, of course, is now plying his damaging trade with Norwich City, who pursued us with resilience and determination all the way to the championship. But, hand on heart, he was the one I didn't want to leave. He grew impatient waiting for his first team guarantee - something I couldn't offer him - and forced the issue. It was always assumed that when Mark wasn't in the team, the bottom line reason was that I didn't fancy him as a player. Quite the opposite was the truth. He might, in fact, have been just the player to win us the title the season Leeds nipped through on the run-in. He could sniff out a goal better than most and I appreciated that asset as well as anybody in the game. But there was a problem. From the December of that campaign right through the winter months, until the virtual death throes when Leeds became champions, Robins was injured. Because most of the other long-term casualties had recovered I gave permission for Mark to have an operation in April. Sod's law, of course, and we suffered a few more injuries as soon as he was packed off to hospital. With Mark available the options would have been different; and so might the title endgame.

In all honesty, though, I concede that I valued Robins as a life-saver for us far more often when he was employed as a substitute. Invariably, when I picked him for the starting line-up he didn't really seem to perform to any satisfactory level. Free him from the bench in the second half and he could terrify opposition teams with his penalty-area awareness. In that fill in role he could be brilliant. But I could understand Mark's point of view. He wanted to be recognised as a first team regular not, as he saw it, a part-timer. He didn't want to be labelled supersub like Liverpool's David Fairclough a few years before. I understood his point of view.

My dilemma was obvious. I had a young lad banging at my door who, in my judgement, was not really a full-time competitor to dislodge Mark Hughes or Brian McClair. They were never injured, always competed in all attacking areas, and scored a reasonable ration of goals. If Robins played, one of them had to go,

Mark Robins - "blessed with the capacity to score goals out of nothing"

and I wasn't prepared to jettison either of my top pairing. But I didn't want their young rival departing the building either. I repeatedly emphasised to Mark that I wasn't in any desperate hurry to sell him, but he was adamant. If he had been prepared to show patience, I advised that in the long-term his ambitions might easily be realised at United. Sadly, for us, Mark reckoned he would just stagnate if he hung around. He decided he had to leave, Norwich came up with the right offer after he had rejected an offer from Germany, and that was it.

But I acknowledge that the Old Trafford crowd took him to their hearts because he was blessed with the capacity to score goals out of nothing. Instinctively, he knew how to finish, an expert in football's own deadly art. I don't mind admitting that I would have Robins back tomorrow if he accepted the role of a squad player with us. I won't ever ignore, or forget, the huge contribution he made in that famous Cup tie victory at Forest that literally set the ball rolling for me as a successful United manager. I can still vividly recall the flood at Hereford when Noah might have been a better bet as our saviour even though we were happy to settle for a combination of Mike Duxbury and Clayton Blackmore. The tremendous, soul-stirring atmosphere of Newcastle, too. And possibly as much as anything the fact that we overcame a horrendous catalogue of injuries to senior players that season.

Liverpool, under Graeme Souness, when they had casualty worries last season, collected the kind of sympathy you normally expect only from the Salvation Army. They weren't, I assure you, any worse than ours in 1990.

When we reached the FA Cup semi-final against Oldham, for example, I played both Bryan Robson and Neil Webb. Neither had more preparation than three or four work-outs in junior games after very lengthy absences through injury. Neil had in fact been missing all that season after his Achilles tendon snapped playing for England in Sweden. To give them the beckoning finger at that point was a calculated gamble. Oldham were on a roll, a very exciting, free-running team that took attacking risks themselves. But I figured the mere presence of Robson and Webb, both players of international stature, would be a powerful psychological threat no matter what they achieved with the ball.

They proved immensely helpful in moving our bandwagon down the road to Wembley even though neither was much more than half fit. Character and courage count for as much as skill in that kind of situation. They showed me for the first time the chink of daylight at the end of a tunnel of gloom, even if I still felt surrounded by dangerous circumstances. I knew I was safe; the problem was that the trouble-mongers refused to believe it until I had that first trophy firmly in my grip.

*"Motivation is all about firing
a person's inner feelings,
inspiring qualities they can't
reach for themselves."*

CHAPTER FIVE

Once Bitten, Twice Shy

**When a long-chased football achievement slips through your fingers, it is
inevitably a cruel and agonising moment. But some experiences can also burn a
scar in a sportsman's soul as an indelible reminder that no cause is ever lost.**

Not forever, anyway. Liverpool, in the spring of 1992, was just such an
experience for United. History will mark it as the scene of our championship
disaster. I'll record it, no question at all, as the day we discovered exactly what
we needed to do to conquer antagonism, hostility, even downright envy, to
become the team that mattered. Because on that day we grew into men. Men
who could win. Might sound corny, but it's true.

Now I fully appreciate that Anfield is hardly the stadium where the home fans
are going to plant garlands round our necks and a welcoming kiss on both cheeks!
It's very much enemy territory, and fiercely defended at that. But that bitter
experience, as Leeds, a hundred miles or so across the Pennines, were toasting our
misery in title champagne, was a very hard lesson on the learning curve.

It's easy for me to relate blow by blow the countdown of events in the six hours of that particular afternoon. From their armchair grandstands, the nation saw Leeds beat Sheffield United, us lose to Liverpool, and the championship trophy marked post haste for Elland Road. A nice, neat package if you happened to be Howard Wilkinson. Privately though I witnessed a lot more. So did my players. And they were memories that drove them inexorably forward a year later when we reached eagerly to seize that very same crown.

We knew that Liverpool's players would not do us any favours. That day, any day most probably, they wanted to beat us more than any other team in the world. And they managed it with a couple of goals that must have made the earth move for most Scousers. Take my word for it - it didn't take long for the gloating to start. Or the four letter taunts to start flying from their camp about my United being thwarted again. We took that sort of dressing-room stick,

Scouse grouse

turned our backs and walked out. That's when we bumped into something I certainly didn't expect.

Liverpool fans taunting Kanchelskis after our defeat

Groups of Liverpool fans gathered around our players. They asked for autographs. No problem at all, even though we were as sick as the proverbial parrots. Then came the nasty little twist. As the United lads handed over the signed mementoes, those same supporters simply tore them up right in their faces and let the litter fall to the floor. What a class act! I spotted Lee Sharpe and Paul Ince sitting together and urged them both: "Remember this day and just how important you are at Manchester United. What has just happened should tell you all how much people envy you. They wouldn't have done that otherwise. It proves how big we are."

So, even though a few chins were on the floor, there was that vital lesson to absorb for the future. It would come in very handy, I was sure of that. Because it was an experience that could only make each one of them better, stronger, more defiant. Provide us with a cause that stirred the blood - something which I have mentioned already as being the key to any significant success. If somebody is trying to do you down a jungle instinct takes over - the only thought in your head is to give them a nasty bite back, and quickly. So that's exactly what we did. Once we returned to Anfield, roughly ten months later and with another championship focused in our sights, we were in the mood to have Liverpool ducking for any available cover. We didn't have Eric Cantona, but on that sweet occasion it didn't matter. We beat them 2-1 and, you know what, we didn't have too many requests for autographs from Anfield's fans after that match. I don't think of it now in terms of cold-hearted revenge, but a demonstration of hardened resolve from United players who had been down a hard road the year before. This time they weren't going to end up in the ditch.

Secret fears   In the previous season, when the whole title outcome was fixed for a double Sunday showdown, I had long suspected our own challenge might end in tears. Obviously I had not breathed a word of my secret worries to the players. But they had been planted in my mind for a month or two. And there was nothing to cushion my fears as the team bus sped towards Anfield with the radio tuned into Leeds United's midday kick-off at Bramall Lane. Leeds got off to a flyer, charging in front, only for Sheffield United to equalise. They missed a couple more - almost heart failure for us - and then it was two each. A life-line perhaps, but we only clung to it briefly before Leeds snatched another goal. I knew then, before we had kicked a ball in anger, it was all over.

But I was still fully committed to a death or glory finale. For me, it had to be a case of the big game, big name syndrome and I tossed both Robson and Ince in to drive the midfield, even though they weren't quite combat-ready. My thinking was that Liverpool, fired by the motivation that we were the last champions they wanted in England, would be more concerned about the presence of our big two than anybody else. Even though we ended up losing, I was immensely proud of the way all my players coped with difficult circumstances. We hit the inside of the post, rattled the bar for good measure, and Liverpool's second goal came via a breakout. So, after all the drama of a season that promised everything, I found myself sitting through a stirring last reel, but one without a happy ending.

"Losing my temper is just part of the way I do my job"

Mind you, I had been squirming on the touchline for a while. First I suffered a touch of the championship wobbles against our sworn enemy, Manchester City, a few weeks earlier - only a gut feeling, but those instinctive inner reactions can often tell you so much. And I was getting serious vibes then that we might not win the title despite being favourites with most football followers and certainly the bookies. City had just turned over the big challengers, Leeds, 4-0 at Maine Road, which shook me up a bit. The grapevine was intimating that most of the Leeds players felt in their hearts they had blown their chance that day, which was encouraging, but I knew it was our turn the following midweek.

The date, engraved on my heart ever since, was April 6th. Smack in the middle of our preparations for the League Cup final with Nottingham Forest. The focus was strictly on City; they were very much heading the priority list as far as I was concerned and for a while it was a cruise. We were one up and so superior it was almost embarrassing. Then their full back Neil Poynton was sent off after an incident with Ryan Giggs. The old red card was more like a red rag for City. They roused themselves and the roof fell in when Keith Curle's penalty wrapped the game up 1-1. The bad feeling told me we had blown the championship that night. Victory would have taken us nine points clear of Leeds and, certainly at that stage of the run-in, virtually over the horizon and out of sight.

That kind of setback had been nagging inwardly at me for a while. The team would perform well, but not quite achieve the result they deserved. I kept muttering to myself: "I hope we don't regret blowing another one." But we did. And then we came up against opposition you can't possibly beat - cussed old Fate with a capital F decided to put the boot in. We lost six players in seven days through injury. I didn't think it was unreasonable that I should lose my temper once in a while under that sort of pressure. But the press have pages to fill and the incessant Fergie Fury headlines really started bugging me. The subtle implication was that my dressing-room explosions were a fundamental reason for the title slipping away. And sometimes subtle didn't come into it - the accusations were delivered with the bluntness of a blacksmith's hammer. To this day, however, I totally refute that notion that I in any way harmed our chances simply by letting my frustrations out into the open.

The fact is that I have won more than a dozen different trophies as a manager and, furthermore, I have done it by going barmy in the dressing-room and losing my temper if necessary. The media say I'm snapping under pressure and affecting the players. But I call it motivation. How can a team have complete faith in its manager if setbacks that bring them to the brink of despair appear to wash over him without a ripple? My approach at half time has never changed whether we are winning, losing, or whatever the circumstances. Losing my temper is just part of the way I do my job. My task is to correct the team's mistakes, cajole, persuade or bully the players to do better, and trigger the charge of adrenalin for the second half. If I have to have a force eight blast to do it then I will. I have the experience to know my temper is a powerful tool. I've been using it for years and I see little purpose in stopping now.

Motivation is all about firing a person's inner feelings, inspiring qualities they can't reach for themselves. In fifteen minutes of half time that is my principal responsibility. And I defy anyone to demonstrate to me that during that very short period of intense emotion my teams don't respond to my promptings. Whether I'm screaming my head off or whispering a private word. No, it definitely wasn't a question of the so-called Fergie Fury that wrecked United's ambitions at that time. There were certain influential factors beyond our control.

Three of them to be exact. The terrible state of the pitch was one; four games in six days was another crippler; and of course we had the handicap of the huge casualty list that I mentioned. If that combination of problems were ever again to besiege any front-running team in the country, I promise you the very same thing would happen. Their rivals three or four points adrift would catch them every time. And that's exactly what happened to us when high expectation turned into total misery. I might smile, I might scowl, but there was little I could do about it.

Deliberately I resisted making changes and tinkering with the team. Admittedly, I left Mark Hughes out in a crucial game we lost against Forest. Aye, *that* damn team again! But it was an option I decided to rely on simply for tactical purposes. The scouting intelligence was that Nigel Clough was going to operate at centre-back alongside Des Walker. The defensive equation was easy to fathom. Clough would be detailed to pick up Sparky while Walker, their fast interceptor, would attempt to take care of Ryan Giggs. I felt that Hughes' style of holding up the ball and feeding runners would suit Clough. He's not quick, not even really mobile, so I decided we needed attackers who would dodge round and get in behind him. I considered deploying Lee Sharpe and Ryan Giggs through the middle to upset him. But in the end I opted for Brian McClair, a player who is always in perpetual motion and never easy to mark. He sneaked about, forced a remarkable save from goalkeeper Mark Crossley, and as a team we played pretty well. The result didn't show it - we lost 2-1. But the memory of that match stuck with us a long time. It might even be said that it literally hung over us for a large part of the championship season.

Descent into Hell

Let me explain. During the summer break, with the team and myself still licking a few private wounds, a specially framed photograph from a United sympathiser was dropped into Old Trafford. For all of us it was like a still from a horror movie: the split-second when Steve Bruce climbed for that soaring header against Forest, the one he couldn't miss, the one he put wide of the post. I'm not surprised the photograph had been captioned 'Dante's Inferno', but it was brilliant all the same.

Instantly, the camera had been focused on the United bench and the supporters surrounding us. The expressions on so many faces were just incredible. I had my head in my hands, Robbo and Mike Phelan looked as though the taxman had just knocked on the door, our physio Jimmy McGregor

Brian McClair - "always in perpetual motion"

was in a trance - it was just amazing. The perfect picture of a back-up team being tortured, reduced to helpless onlookers unable to do a solitary thing to change a calamitous situation. So I decided to hang that picture on a nail in our dressing-room for all the first team to see when they reported back for the new campaign.

The basic reason was to remind every single player of a bad experience, a critical phase when the title started sliding down the pan, and make certain it never haunted them again. It stayed there for weeks. Then, mysteriously, the photograph vanished when we were having another rough spell in October. The psychological point had been made, anyway, and I could understand why the players wanted it packing away in a trunk. You can take only so much with a nightmare memory.

But the ordeal of losing to Leeds certainly steeled us and helped tremendously in preparing us for the weeks of tension when Aston Villa pursued us to the wire. The whole experience, I have not the slightest doubt, gave us a distinct advantage. You know you are inextricably locked in a war of nerves. That's what it's all about. How you keep a firm grip of discipline and temperament is vital. If you succumb to the twitch you are finished. I suspected we were more prepared, hardened to the job than Villa, and I believe history proved me right.

The common theme in the press box at the time was that Ron's side had more championship background and expertise than we had. It was a weak argument. Sure, they had Ray Houghton and Steve Staunton, who had been all the way with Liverpool, and their skipper Kevin Richardson had the rare distinction of being a champion with two different clubs, Everton and Arsenal. But count them up, three out of eleven, and there were eight innocents left to work into the equation. And Ron had never been down the championship road either. Not as close to the pressure cooker as I had been the year before.

You instinctively understand how to avoid being burned twice. So I knew what to expect and how to shield my players from the dangers that run through the head as well as those that undermine a defence on the field. The lesson in being a loser was painful, but it was certainly understood and learned very well. It's just like being directed to a town you have never visited before. Once you have been along the route, discovered how to avoid the traffic snarl-ups and the roads that lead nowhere, the journey becomes far easier second time around. Consequently, in March, April and May of 1993, I felt a lot more comfortable about our prospects than I had a year earlier. But also I had a pretty good idea of the emotions and fears that were circulating in the Villa camp at the same time. The signs were there for everyone to see.

When they arrived at Old Trafford for our big game, there was a classic giveaway. Ron and his Villa backroom team stood about in the corridor outside their dressing-room laughing and joking. They tried to present the appearance of being a bunch of blokes preparing for a holiday. No sweat, this one - just another ordinary day at the office. You must be joking, I thought. To me it was quite clear that this was a calculated act of bravado for the benefit of their players. The sort of psychological trickery I wouldn't be averse to myself! Just looking at their little act, I instantly knew they were feeling the pain and anxiety of the whole situation. Life can never be a picnic when played out at the level of competition we were at. They were putting on a show because we were the team that could inflict most damage on their high hopes. Footballers see through that kind of business anyway and I knew that the resolve of my own players had been tempered and hardened by real life experience twelve months earlier. That was our edge.

Late, late show

The nail in Villa's coffin, no question, was our late, late show against Sheffield Wednesday. I had watched them just before that fixture when they had played Spurs and the clear indication was that they were suffering from goal starvation. Tottenham had just survived the epic, pitch-invasion Cup tie with Manchester City and were clearly paying for it. They were happy to sit back and contain. Villa shuddered the post a couple of times but, those chances apart, never looked like creating a threat. Their swagger and confidence seemed to be vanishing fast. Next for them was Coventry and a goal-less draw.

Steve Bruce - "rescuing us in the nick of time"

They must have been soaking in the bath at Villa Park, soothing muscles and aching hearts with the knowledge that Wednesday had us in trouble. When Villa's final whistle blew we were one-nil down. As the record book proves Steve Bruce was our rescuer that day with two fantastic goals, one very late in the second half and the winner six minutes into overtime. They stirred controversy and, in my opinion, a great deal of unnecessary fuss. As I mentioned earlier, the referee short-changed us that day. We should have played at least four minutes longer than we did.

I monitored the whole game from the video and the time check proves that we lost 12 minutes of play during the 90 minutes. For a start, Michael Peck, the referee who hurt himself in the match, received treatment for three-and-a-half minutes. Wednesday had the physio on the field when Viv Anderson, John Sheridan and Carlton Palmer went down and Peter Schmeichel and Brucie were also injured. Four substitutions also had the watch ticking on and yet we actually played just an extra seven and half minutes. The ref, in fact, blew up almost as soon as we knocked in the winner. He might just as well have tootled on a victory trumpet as well because that single result was so decisive in winning the championship.

At times like that vivid pictures of the past flash through the mind. I remembered with a shudder down my spine the absolute devastation when we lost it the year before. It was an ordeal for everybody involved. Of course, we are all equipped with that inbuilt, protective mechanism that seems to foresee what's going to happen. The way things were panning out then told me it wasn't to be fairy tale time. Little by little, game by game, I came to terms with our fate. You have to be logical and totally realistic because life is not going to end with losing a title.

For managers the immediate reaction is to protect their players from too much emotional fallout. You must repair their damage because your own scars are really inconsequential. Far more important is the future of the team and I was blessed with one I knew could come back. The black border would soon turn into our silver lining. So after that crushing day at Liverpool I barely uttered a word to the first team squad. I just allowed everything to seep into their souls and let them get on with handling the huge disappointment of it all.

A shoulder to cry on

But for the last match against Spurs I decided the time of mourning was over. We needed the right send-off for the summer break. I ordered the champagne be put on ice and set out in the dressing-room. Sir Matt and all the directors were given the summons to join us. And the celebration, even if we were considered public losers, was swinging as the fans poured out of Old Trafford to fix their ambitions on another season. I told the whole assembly: "The title has gone to Leeds and yet we had 46,000 packed into the ground for the last game of the season. Just think about it. At any other place in the country they would be burning the stadium to the ground if that happened. Those people love you and you have repaid them with some terrific performances over the last few months. We have won the League Cup and the Super Cup. All we need to do is gather strength and make sure we are all together to have another right go at it next season."

Mind you, I pinched myself before I launched into that little speech. I needed to. How can you talk about what a good season it's just been when the title has been ripped from your grasp? But I reasoned that somewhere along the line you have to stop wallowing in all the misery and self-pity. We knew we hadn't deserved our fate - and that's exactly what had stopped us: *Fate*. That season there were simply factors beyond the control of even a very impressive and gifted side. Apart from the

"After that crushing day at Liverpool I just allowed everything to seep into their souls."

fixture log-jam, injuries and the Old Trafford pitch, Leeds must have been smacking their lips when we knocked them out of both Cup competitions so early in the action. We went to Elland Road three times in nine days and produced some fabulous individual performances.

After driving back from that day of destiny at Liverpool there were umpteen factors that sprang to mind as I mulled over the season with my brother Martin - and a bottle of wine to ease the agony of it all. Up until Christmas, I confirmed to myself, that team - with Robson controlling things - had scored goals, and they had also played with as much excitement and flourish as we did in winning it in '93. The ultimate killer was that programme of four matches in six days. Rambo

Peter Schmeichel - "ready to win it next time"

couldn't have handled that.

But the consolation was that I was convinced we still had the players good enough and young enough to win it next time round. Peter Schmeichel had revealed his outstanding assets as a goalkeeper in his first season, and I knew he would continue to improve. So would Ryan Giggs and Gary Pallister. And Ince, as I have mentioned earlier, was maturing as a creative player and a strong personality. It needn't be all dark clouds and pessimism once a common sense, emotion-free assessment took over from all the tears and disappointment.

Next time we would do it - I could feel a title coming on.

"I've nursed him through the teenage years, seen him over the bumps and bruises of life, seen him grow as a player and develop as a person. Now I hope we are on the verge of celebrating something extremely special at the club."

CHAPTER SIX

Boy Wonder

Ryan Giggs is the most precious, skill-blessed player I have ever had in almost twenty years in management. There is no question about that. He is so gifted that when Ryan was just 14, Bobby Charlton would book himself a day off from work simply to watch him in schoolboy games. When he was not much older, United's biggest names would stand in awe on the touchline and goggle at him like fans. And that was just while he was going through his training regimes. Maybe that little testimony will explain why we treat young Ryan like the Crown jewels on legs. Who wouldn't?

For us he is a priceless talent, literally. Twice during our championship summer I firmly and instantly rejected offers of £10 million. They came via a middle-man from AC Milan. The first call was put straight through to me not long after we finished the season and were still on a high with our title celebrations. The cash bid was admittedly a bit mind-boggling but I had one reply: "Fat chance, just forget it." And I put the phone down.

But the Italians aren't just rich, they are persistent as well. Before we kicked off

"He can spin, turn, and change direction so quickly, always with the ball at his feet and under the tightest control."

this season the same wheeler-dealer was back again. The offer was still ten million. Once again my answer was no. I couldn't believe the guy.

"Alex," he pleaded, "this will ruin my credibility in football in Italy. I have never failed to get the player they wanted before." Tough.

"This is Manchester United you're talking to, not some bottom of the table outfit," I replied, and ended the call. But I couldn't help chuckling over his bare-faced cheek because we wouldn't sell. And still won't. Not for double the price. Some day in the future, I accept, Ryan himself might want to take the road to foreign football. But I don't just hope that won't happen; I don't see why it should ever become an issue for a club of our dimensions. So far we have managed to persuade Eric Cantona, a player of global stature, to stay in this country instead of opting for a high-powered European team. Mark Hughes was brought back from Barcelona and in the mid-eighties Bryan Robson in his pomp ignored Juventus and signed a seven-year contract at Old Trafford. I think you'll agree he doesn't appear to have suffered too much for his decision.

So I don't foresee a problem with Giggs. He will, of course, not have to resolve any dilemma himself until his next contract is due when he's 23. Then he might need to sit down and quietly ask himself a few pertinent questions. Like, would it be worth it going to Italy and being subjected to the daily harassment and aggro that appears to plague Paul Gascoigne? Could he achieve anything more over there than he would at United? Would foreign football bring out the best in him and be a true test of his character and ability? Would he benefit from the experience, apart from in financial terms?

What Ryan wants

Certainly if you're talking money, the Italians can offer the kind of financial rewards that are beyond even a huge club like United. And we British tend to gather like magpies when there is mention of any tax-lenient cash on the table. But is there such a huge difference between the sort of lucrative wages that can turn you into a multi-millionaire and being a straightforward millionaire at 23? Because I believe that kind of status is waiting just around the corner for Giggsy already. He mustn't neglect to look at the other side of life and reflect on whether United are the team he dreamt they would be when he was just a boyhood fan. The team he always wanted to play for. If they are, should he be tempted to leave the attraction of all that behind him?

There aren't many stadiums in the world, for instance, that can equal the splendour of Old Trafford. I agree there are great sporting arenas in Spain and Italy, but I don't think any compare with the sense of theatre you are guaranteed at our place. It's hard to match. Certainly it would have to be one of Italy's top three clubs that could present Giggs with anything to come close to it. Part of the foreign equation, and a point to be seriously considered by any footballer in the export market, is that not too many British players find it comfortable or are able to adjust to the Italian game. Only recently there have been classic examples in Ian Rush and Des Walker. Beyond doubt there is proof for Ryan, if he only cares to take a look, that it's not all about mega money and living on Easy Street.

What are his aims after all? His aims include winning major trophies and he can do that here with United. Not too far into the future he will realise the

Ryan Giggs - "What are his aims?"

enormity of this club, just how big we are in the world game. He will understand exactly the role United have played in shaping his destiny and what we can still achieve for him. Another understandable aim is to end his playing career wealthy and without a worry for the rest of his life and I believe we can achieve that for him, too. He's well down that particular road even now. So what else can Ryan want? There's maybe a curiosity about sampling what foreign soccer is all about. But that's something really to be considered when he is in his mid-twenties. When the stardust has gone and he can make a mature and proper decision for himself.

There are so many imponderables for Ryan, but thankfully he doesn't really need to examine his career planning or ambitions too closely for two or three years yet. There is no point to it. No point in adding to the speculation, no point in anyone making silly bids, and no point in the lad himself even thinking about it. He appreciates he is still learning his trade and is not mature or experienced enough to consider such a massive step. But, more than anything else, there is the small factor that he is not for sale. Not at any price. The question is not even on the United agenda. Get the message?

Star attraction   You can't blame the major foreign clubs for being drawn like moths to a flame. Not even they can breed a footballer of Ryan's calibre; his ability is heaven sent. They pop up maybe once in a couple of generations and almost stop the world when they turn on the magic.

Just such a moment was that stunning goal from Giggs on September 19, 1992, at Tottenham. Remember the one? It was shown, week in week out, as the spectacular come-on while the theme music drew us all to our armchairs for "Match of the Day" last season. I'll never forget it, I know that. Poetry in motion, you might say - a touch of sheer class that's almost indefinable.

Step by step, let me take you through the whole sequence. For a start Dean Austin, Spurs' young full back that day, made a fatal error and failed to control the ball properly. You don't do that with Giggs in the area; it's like inviting Jaws for dinner in the local swimming baths. He's so quick, if you blink you miss him. Their boy half slips and that's it. Ryan's got the ball now, takes it up to him, slips it through poor Austin's legs and away. I swear that he ducked through the legs himself - others tell me that really he hurdled over the top of him. Aye, hellfire, it was so good I call that nit-picking!

Anyway, don't spoil the story. Next in line is Jason Cundy, their big centre back. Sees Giggsy is through, so he comes across to intercept. That's my ball, you can see him thinking. Sorry, son, no you don't, and Ryan - cheeky little chap - nicks it through his legs as well. Neil Ruddock is caught square by the impudence of it all and is out of the game. That's what happened with Tottenham in those days. They always tried to play offside, so if you beat one centre-back by going past him you automatically beat the other one as well. Sorry, forget the diversion, and

"That's my ball," thinks Jason Cundy, but Ryan has other ideas

get back to the real business. Giggsy's goal in a million... Their 'keeper, Ian Walker, is next up. And he clearly thinks he is going to get the ball as well. Commits himself and it's "Goodnight Vienna". Ryan ghosts round him, the net is waiting, and he puts it away without breaking sweat. It was a split-second before half time and it must have ruined the meat pies and cuppas for the home fans on Tottenham's terraces. On reflection, I'm pretty sure they could react only one way and reach for the simple consolation that there was only a single player on that pitch who could have scored such a majestic goal. Live until you're ninety and you won't see one better. It was off the planet, a truly outstanding sequence of creative football with a finish to match. World class.

He's a defender's worst nightmare. It's chilling the way Ryan seems to float over the surface rather than run like the rest of us. His United team-mates swear he doesn't touch the ground like us mere mortals when he is powering forward but, instead, kind of misses a beat in his stride. So light on his feet and blessed with wonderful, wonderful balance. I can't stress that quality too much. He is so quick and checks with that instant stop that makes you think he was born with an ABS braking system in his feet. Whatever the secret, markers just can't live with him. They are falling all over the place and he is still on his feet ready for the next one. Ryan will run and check, run and check, until the white hankie is waved by the opposition in surrender.

Float like a butterfly

I suspect the best man to question on the subject of Giggs is our own former player, Viv Anderson. When Viv was still with us, Ryan was no more than fifteen and we had fixed him to play with the top men in a practice match at The Cliff training complex. Viv, remember, was an experienced England international, a well proven full back who had played all around the world against some of the top attackers you care to name. And he hadn't seen many like Giggs, that's for certain. He was soon on the wrong end of a very torrid time, looking at the rest of us and asking: "What the hell is going on here? Who is this?" Suddenly, Viv, a great old pro who didn't want to do anything nasty to a young, wet-nosed kid, figured he had better do something about it. One or two tackles started flying about and, believe me, it all turned a bit serious.

But did it all get to Ryan? Not a bit of it. Physically, he might not look much but he can certainly take care of himself on the park. When he looks your way on the pitch, he fixes you with those cold, unblinking eyes. They bore through you like lasers. No, there ain't anybody going to make him twitch and tremble while he's wearing football boots. There is a soldier's courage in him and he is also as strong as a bull. He might look like a little boy lost at times, not much more than ten stone nine wet through. But, mentally and physically, he is armour-plated, a very tough cookie indeed.

Small beginnings

My first glimpse of Ryan was when he was even smaller, just a wisp of a kid in fact, during my first Christmas at the club in 1986. As soon as he ran out on the training field, head proudly in the air, you could see he was a player. He presented me with an immediate mental picture that I have kept to this day. It was like watching one of those little cocker spaniels chasing a piece of floating, wind-blown waste paper around the park. You know what I mean. They have their heads in the air, dancing in a dozen different directions, their eyes fixed on the paper and pursuing it all over the place. That was Ryan. He can spin, turn, and change direction so quickly, always with the ball at his feet and under the tightest control. At the time I just muttered to myself: "Jeez, we've got some player here."

Our players used to line up when they had finished their training sessions and watch him doing his tricks. Beaten-up old pros, who think they have seen and done it all, don't hang around too often like that. It's got to be something special to keep them out of the showers for long. And, as I have mentioned before, even a football figure of the stature of Bobby Charlton could barely believe what he was witnessing in a player at such a young age. He would always call me to check on the schoolboy fixtures to discover exactly when Giggs was playing. Then he would make certain he had a day off work to watch him in action. It should tell you everything for a man with Bobby's world-wide business considerations to mould his schedule around a young kid like that.

Giggs - "A very exciting, highly-skilled rookie"

He appreciates, like the rest of us at United, that we are seeing a rare, rare talent. But it's a highly risky proposition making judgements and predictions when you are dealing with a footballer who is just 19. All you can promise is that Giggs, granted the fortune and good grace his commitment deserves, has every chance of being truly world class. That status will only be recognised throughout our business once he has succeeded at the highest level in a European Cup Final for United, or on the testing stage of the

World Cup finals for his country. In another four or five years we will all discover, Ryan included, how far he can develop and what sort of impact he can make on the global game. Considered in those sort of terms, what we are witnessing now is a very exciting, highly skilled rookie.

At the moment it's all about exploring a seam of fabulously rich potential. Sometimes you see in Ryan incredible maturity, football quality far beyond his years. Then, a match or two later, he might reveal an irritating glimpse of youthfulness and naivety about the game. That's to be expected. With kids you can never achieve, or rightly expect, perfect balance and consistency in their football. In one instant Ryan can have you leaping off the stadium seat and next he is guilty of a novice's mistake that you would never anticipate. But experience of the game has taught me to expect that sort of contrast. Maturity and fulfilling potential are essentially one and the same thing. Some players never, in fact, achieve their potential and what you see in them at, say twenty, is all you are going to get. To be blunt, they never grow up.

But what I already quite clearly recognise in Ryan is the greatest talent I have ever been asked to manage. So, naturally, it's vitally important that I make it work. It places you in a position of tremendous responsibility but also grants the rare privilege that every manager works all his life to attain: producing a world-class footballer. No, maybe that's overstepping the mark, because I can't genuinely claim I have produced Giggs. But what I can say is that I have helped to mould and shape the natural assets with which he kicked off his career.

I've nursed him through the teenage years, seen him over the bumps and bruises of life in the growing-up process. I've given him stick, had him wash down my car when all he wanted was to dart off and play snooker, watched him sweeping out the dressing-rooms, doing all the menial tasks. You have seen Ryan grow as a player and develop as a person, which is just as important. Now, I hope that we are on the verge of celebrating something extremely special at the club. Once that landmark of full maturity is achieved, when all the high expectations have been realised, it's going to be a day of great satisfaction for me. For the coaches, all the people who have helped him along the way, his team-mates and, probably more than anybody, for Ryan himself.

At that moment we can put him on a plinth of his own and applaud him as a role model for future United generations. This club has been blessed with some of the finest home-produced footballers anywhere, including Norman Whiteside, George Best, Mark Hughes and Bobby Charlton. It's always been part of the Old Trafford heritage and sporting culture to be successful on that side of the game. Equally, the transfer market has been an important factor down the decades with the recruitment of Denis Law, Tommy Taylor before him, and more recently Bryan Robson, Paul Ince and Roy Keane. Terrific buys all of them.

But when you unearth a gem like Giggs, see him at thirteen and then watch him putting the best in their places a few seasons later, it gives you a really warm glow. That kind of progress is essentially the kick you get from the management business. The raw material of individual brilliance and instinctive balance and tricks can't be coached into any player. As they all say, he has either got it or he hasn't. But even the most gifted like Giggs can still be taught an awful lot about football. Even now we are heavily involved with him in what we call perceptive work. In other words, trying to improve his soccer sixth sense of total awareness.

Growing up on the pitch

A hiccup on the learning curve cropped up in our Charity Shield victory over Arsenal. For once Giggsy was having a ropey time out there at Wembley. The harder he tried, the worse he became. So I decided to pull him off. You should have seen the black look he gave me. Enough to freeze you to the spot. He just detests that beckoning finger telling him he is being substituted; hates it as though it is an affront to his ability. But occasionally even potentially great players need well-timed reminders about their job. That day Giggs was struggling by his own high standards until the sheer frustration of it all virtually left him chasing his own shadow. It was time for a word of advice.

"Being a young player," I assured him later, "and having a poor match on a big stage was a bit too much for you. You didn't know how to handle it. The answer was to play a simple game, but you had neither the experience nor patience to understand that.

"Of course, Ryan, you're are blessed with an amazing talent. What it means is that individually you want to do better than the last time every time you get the ball. There's nothing wrong with that either. But you have to grow up and discover that you can't manage that every match. Sometimes the ball doesn't run too kindly for you. When you realise it's not going to be quite your day, there is an option - pass it. You've got to say then that I'm going to stay on the touchline for this one and give the opposition problems from there. Draw them in and pass. Make sure the attacks are going to start in that area and, instead of trying to run them ragged, pick out the other runners with a good ball. Everybody has a bad game; what really matters is how you make the best of it. Right, son?"

"Giggsy having a ropey time out there at Wembley"

He has to discover the secret of seeing the big picture out on the park. The innate understanding of how the game changes dramatically when you can lift the heads of all your comrades, inspire a team the way players like Eric Cantona and Glenn Hoddle do. When you have picked up on the secret it's as simple as flicking the TV remote from off to on. You can suddenly see every corner of the pitch and give others the impression there are eyes in the back of your head. It's called awareness. With that quality, the opposition can put three markers on you and you can still inflict a tremendous amount of damage. You can actually kill a team with one pass.

I always like reminding Giggs of John Barnes when he was at his peak.

Naturally we all admired him for the way he could run, beat an opponent or two and then cross a ball. But what impressed me more than anything was the manner in which Barnes could pass balls through any defence very accurately. That was what made him really menacing. Just when you were expecting him to run straight at the full back, he would duck inside and deliver that devastating ball. Aimed right at the heart. So that's one aspect Giggs must necessarily add to his game. Another is the art of the clinical finisher. I'm not attempting to be over-critical, just objective.

Because what we are all seeing at this moment is only part fulfilment of the Giggs potential. In percentage terms it's difficult to determine exactly how much. But I know that for him to become outstanding, an all-time great in world football, he must now improve his vision and passing technique. Take a lesson from history and recall Pelé, when he spotted the 'keeper off his line and from at least 60 yards range had a pop at goal. Or the other occasion when the Brazilian legend dreamed up a dummy as cute as could be, with the ball passing one side of the 'keeper while he dodged the other way. Such is the soccer intelligence that transforms good players into gods.

"Individual brilliance and instinctive balance"

I've suggested to Ryan he might borrow a video and marvel at the uncanny passing ability of Franz Beckenbauer. Franz brought such arrogance, authority and composure to the game, both in defence and attack. All factors that a young player doesn't instinctively have. The swiftness and intelligence of Johann Cruyff or the guile and perception of his Dutch successor, Ruud Gullit, who was prepared to underscore his own greatness by also working harder than anybody else in the team. If Ryan wants to reach that extra footballing dimension he must acquire all the qualities I have listed.

Sharing a dream

He has his dream and I have mine and now I can't wait to see the finished article. It will be like watching a ship being built, taking shape month after month, and then slipping down into the Clyde. Just a fantastic feeling. I'll know the precise moment when we can show Giggs to the whole world and say: "Just take an eyeful at this little lot. All made in Britain, too." With precisely that in mind I have spent my days since winning the championship praying that Wales, even more than England, book themselves a place in the World Cup finals of 1994. They have so many outstanding players, like Ian Rush, Neville Southall, Sparky Hughes and Gary Speed as well as Giggs, that it would be a tragedy if they never played at the very pinnacle of the international game.

The other tragedy I have been determined to avoid, as the frustrated media will only too willingly verify, is that of Giggs being destroyed before he could even stretch forward to possible greatness. They have accused me of keeping the bird of paradise in a gilded cage. The real question to be addressed is whether my entrenched position in protecting Giggs from an avalanche of Press and TV attention has been right. My prime concern was the clear risk of a repetition of the George Best scenario from the sixties or a Gazza syndrome of more recent times. I knew what I had to do; I bolted the Old Trafford door and made certain Ryan was safe inside.

But at the launching point of the new '93/'94 season the local evening newspaper ran a centre-page spread headlined: "The Enemy Within". It was written quite evidently from the media perspective of the Giggs affair and condemned me for shielding him from the attentions of outsiders. The charge was that I was being over protective and molly-coddling the boy too much.

Can Ryan take Wales to World Cup glory?

Consequently, the article maintained, I was in effect inviting an invasion of his privacy. *I* had to take the criticism, *I* was wholly to blame, according to them. It was an attack that admittedly made me very angry. There is nobody in their right minds at United, nobody in possession of any feelings for the boy, who would ever level that kind of accusation at me. But I'm not against self-analysis on such delicate issues. I gave a lot of thought to it, tossed the obvious questions over in private, and wondered if people were suggesting: "Aye, that's right, he has created a monster out of the situation. He is really the guilty man." They might have weighed things up and adjudged that I had got things wrong and mishandled Giggs' career.

But, even with the benefit of hindsight, I categorically insist I was right all along. If we had allowed open house with Ryan we would have been asking for a state of media anarchy. It would have been bedlam. They would never have left him alone and I'm afraid that he would have been exploited as an innocent victim of the media wars that are now part of our daily lives. We can't change that aspect, or do much to correct it, because it's beyond our control. But we can make sure we don't become too involved by operating, for want of a better description, a self-protection racket. So that's all we have done.

We appreciate we have a potential trouble zone in the sense that we have this young, incredible talent at the club and that every man and his dog wants a part of the action. We say, for the time being, that's just not possible. The emergence of Giggs as a footballer would be seriously handicapped if we allowed it. He would not be granted a moment of peace and quiet. I understand why he is such a magnet. There are not too many of his kind around, but that's not my problem. It doesn't mean we should step back and allow him to be turned into a commercial sideshow for the spin-off merchants.

Consider the case of Gascoigne, for example. There has been literally a media explosion around him over the last couple of years. Sure, to some degree, Gazza has been responsible for some of it. Maybe even a party to it as well, so you can hardly condemn most of the ballyhoo as sheer exploitation. But that doesn't escape the fact that the media are drawn compulsively to Gazza and I wanted to avoid that three-ring circus routine with Giggs. The no-go areas have been rigidly policed by me and he has been free to get on with being a footballer. There's plenty of time for Ryan to develop into a full-blown, upfront personality later in his life when he has the maturity to cope with it all. My firm intention is that he won't fall victim to that infamous trap of British sporting life: the toppling of our idols. It seems to be a perverse part of our nature in these islands that when we are blessed with a great talent, eventually we try to destroy it. In certain commercial elements you see it. They simply want to pull down the legend, break it apart and shatter the person inside. George Best was a prime example and one of the earliest to suffer for it as well. The lesson was learned the hard way at this club and it's an illustration that we now use with young players' parents in promising we will make sure no one else is lured down a wayward path.

George Best, of course, was a part of the massive cultural change in the swinging sixties. That was the decade when social and family values were altered dramatically; it was the watershed of the post-war era. Flower power, Beatlemania, the anything-goes generation, a mood of complete liberation. And Besty, good-looking personality and so gifted he was a footballing freak, was swept up in the hysteria of it all. But I think nowadays even he would confess

The gagging of Giggsy

that he couldn't handle all of that side of his life. It almost suffocated him and, arguably, drove him out of football earlier than he would have wished.

Following that experience and, admittedly, dropping George's name as a special reference in the conversation, I assure each parent I see that I will personally make sure their boy is looked after. The treatment of Ryan in this respect is no different from the rest. He just happens to be the biggest goldfish in the bowl. The senior players protect him as much as me. If we ever have to close ranks then we

"The idea is to have Giggs playing at United without a flicker of worry or trauma in his life"

most certainly do. Any adverse reaction from outsiders who don't like what we are doing is, putting it bluntly, just ignored. The idea is to have Giggs playing at United without a flicker of worry or trauma in his life. We don't want him walking round every corner to have a camera rammed in his face. It isn't part of his job to be seen on telly telling the world what he eats for breakfast or what his favourite CD happens to be. The information might be interesting to some folk, but for the life of me I can't think why, and it's certainly of no material value to us as a football club.

presumably a French onion-seller's at that! - leaving us all behind for good.

It's a constant talking point, an issue that never seems to go away. Too right, they argue, he's been brilliant at United, but how long is he going to stay? And so I accept this situation could be my next major dilemma and also something of a watershed in Eric's well-travelled career, too. I'm besieged by people telling me that Cantona moves on all the time, that he has this gypsy in his soul that drives him towards some new adventure every year or so. The imponderable is always there demanding an answer: will he or won't he be here next season - even next week? You want to know how I have learned to handle it? I'll tell you how, by switching off and not actually expecting anything at all beyond the next 24 hours.

The question of Cantona the wanderer is raised so often with me that now I approach it with a single thought. I think if he is here today, tremendous, but if he is gone tomorrow we just say: "Good luck, Eric, thanks for playing for us; you have been absolutely brilliant." But, honestly, we just don't know what's going to happen. We can't get in deeply enough to learn about Eric just yet because he hasn't been here long enough for that. I sincerely hope he will stay around for a while so we might understand exactly what makes him tick. In the meantime it's fingers crossed about a footballer who firmly believes in riding his own destiny.

The open-ended honeymoon

Eric's not the enigma people often suppose, but he is very different from all the other players. Different in his nature, his temperament, his cultural background, almost everything in fact. Little wonder he's not on the same wavelength as the rest of us. This *vive la difference* all wrapped up in the legend of an idiosyncratic footballer-poet is what makes us all very wary of how long our mutual relationship can last. It could be a lengthy honeymoon - who can say? But I have deliberated and have now decided I am not, just for a change, going to get all worked up about it. If it happens that Eric sticks around for a long time, then fantastic, but I don't want to get to the stage where there is any acrimony between us. We want it to be nice and peaceful.

Basically, that's where I have had to change my whole attitude, maybe do a bit of a U-turn on my usual policy, and accept that we have a different type of player around the house. They all say that contracts don't really matter to Eric. That if there is something he wants to attempt or achieve elsewhere there is no stopping him. But so far he has remained dedicatedly loyal to United. He was prepared during his early season injury problems to play for us and risk his World Cup position with France. That underlines for me how much he loves being here. And even if he

France and United's "footballer-poet"

were stricken by the *wanderlust* again he would still have United in his heart. He appreciates exactly what he has achieved at Old Trafford in an extremely short time span.

Jetsetting...

Showing off during the summer tour of South Africa

With coaches from Tembisa township

United supporters in Soweto

Pre-season pep talk for Clayton and Ryan

Working out in the African heat

My favourite pastime!

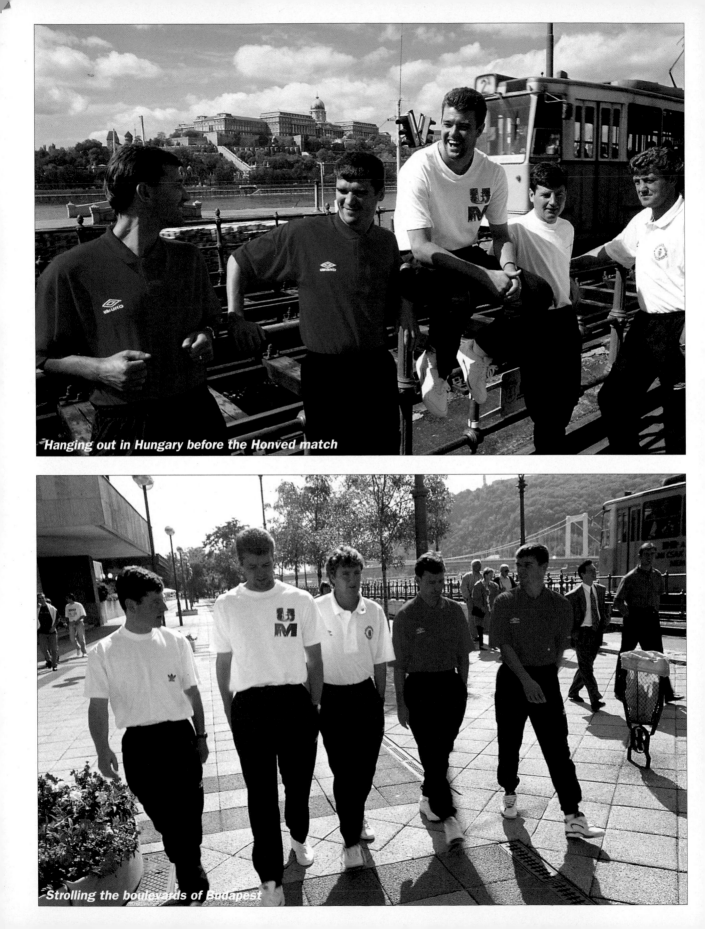

Hanging out in Hungary before the Honved match

Strolling the boulevards of Budapest

Forget how much longer he decides to hang about. In my view Cantona has been well worth the investment, whatever happens in the future. But that should not be interpreted as a case of my being relaxed on the issue. If Eric walked in my office in the morning and explained that he wanted to leave, I would move heaven and earth to keep him. No manager would be more committed to talk him out of that decision than me. Even if we had to sit there until Christmas to do it. I would definitely enlist the assistance of Gerard Houillier, the French national manager, to help me out if necessary.

I might even take our beloved Frenchman to Govan, show him the Clyde, and explain I'm the only man in the world who can get him into heaven! Seriously, though, I would do everything in my power to keep Eric in our team. I would be failing in my job if I didn't try to pull out all the stops. For a start, I would need a complete explanation and detailed reasoning on why he wanted out. A lot of players might have their heads turned by persuasive bundles of money; not Eric. It would need to be a case with him of stirring the soccer soul.

He is already established as an idol on our terraces but, in truth, that wouldn't sway me at all if push came to shove with Eric. Our supporters have plenty of other idols anyway. No, the crucial and deciding factor with me in talking round Cantona, would have to be his achievements with United so far and the prizes he has still to plunder. This is a partnership that shouldn't be surrendered easily. My greatest wish is that he should be enjoying life at United more than he would anywhere else. If that is the case then he will still be here for some time, I know that for certain. So it's my task to make sure he remains happy and content.

Fate knocking

Since the day he arrived in November, 1992, Eric has never given me the slightest hint that he is feeling footloose again. He understands and fully appreciates what we have to offer. The atmosphere, the drama, the electric tension of the place lights him up. Old Trafford is Cantona's spiritual home, no mistake about that. And how he arrived on our doorstep, in a deal that lasted just 25 hours from first call to final signing, was quite incredible, too. I suspect my old friend, Fate, was again involved with a bit of a blind side run to help out.

The scene was the chairman's office on a drizzly day in November. Martin Edwards and myself were running through a target list of top strikers. Our number one choice, England and Sheffield Wednesday forward David Hirst, had to be struck off the list after we heard a telexed offer of £3.5 million received the knock back from an extremely unhappy Trevor Francis. Back to the drawing board so to speak. We knew immediate action was imperative. In thirty five days through October and the start of November the old curse had come back to haunt the team. The goals had dried up. In seven games we hit the net just four times, lost three and drew three. Not good enough. It was like a bad memory returning from the season before.

We nattered on, shuffling through the names, and I mentioned it was a pity we didn't get a sniff a season earlier when Cantona was first brought to this country. The Frenchman, I pondered, might just have been a possibility to test on trial for the rest of that campaign. The sort of arrangement that Leeds had made in fact. Might even have won us the title we lost to them. Then the phone rang and

Martin picked it up. On the other end was Bill Fotherby, the managing director at Elland Road, sounding us out about Denis Irwin. The timing was weird, absolutely uncanny.

They came straight out with it - was Denis for sale? Martin, automatically knowing the answer, glanced across at me: "No chance at all," I reassured him. Then, in whispers and sign language, I tried to prime the conversation about Cantona. Martin didn't get the drift, so I scribbled Eric's name on a scrap of paper and eased it across the desk. Immediately, Martin tuned in and suggested to Bill that the word on the grapevine was that Cantona wasn't too happy at Leeds after some backroom bust-up. Bill pleaded ignorance.

"All the same," continued Martin, "any chance of you selling him and we'd be interested. Need to know pretty quick, mind you, because we have the money for a striker and want to do some business now. If Eric's not available we'll go elsewhere." Bill rang off with the promise that he would consult Howard Wilkinson. I scooted off to Coventry on business, leaving the rest to the chairman. Within the hour, apparently, Leeds were back and the haggling started. My advice before leaving was that Cantona was certainly worth £1.5 million to us.

I started the motorway journey back and the carphone buzzed in my ear. They are a bit 'squidgy' on confidentiality at times, if you know what I mean, so I warned the chairman not to go into names, only figures.

"We've got him," he explained. "How much do you think?" Trying to be realistic, I suggested £1.6 million.

"Wrong." So then I rattled off three or four more attempts. They were all so far off the mark, it was like one of those TV quizzes. Higher, lower, not even close. Eventually the chairman declared the true figure: £1 million. I just couldn't believe it.

"That's an absolute steal," I blurted out. But Martin explained he stuck out and wouldn't pay any more. He reminded me that Cantona had cost Leeds no more than £900,000. Next we fixed it for Eric's French lawyer to fly in and arranged talks for the following day.

I already had a date in the diary. It was a lunch with City boss Peter Reid to do a joint article on the derby match. As they say in all the best reports, at 3.30 pm I made my excuses and left. The promise was that I would be back as fast as possible. Pretty quick it was, too. In less than an hour the deal with Eric was done and dusted, no nit-picking over the cash side, just a straightforward agreement. I headed back to the hotel to see Reidy. He asked me where I had been and I told him:

"Signing Cantona from Leeds." The air was blue - Reidy reckoned I was taking the mickey and his language was unprintable. Eventually though I convinced him. He knew it was a brilliant deal for us.

Leeds off the leash

But after attending the Press conference, I started to get the jitters about the whole business. Not quite panic, but an uncertainty as to whether we had done the right thing. I began worrying about all the controversial stuff being traded around about Eric's past. The dredgers were really on overtime rates. A couple

"He scores goals, creates goals and dreams up little miracles beyond the imagination of most people."

of Leeds players were quoted and a few innuendos started to filter from Elland Road about him. It looked like a fair amount of propaganda to me. It seemed to be a smoke-screen to placate the Leeds fans wondering why one of their favourite players had been sold to a deadly rival.

Eric Cantona - "understands and fully appreciates what we have to offer"

I didn't know how to take it. The situation upset me, but not for more than a few hours. It was then I decided to ignore the whispering campaign. I had bought the player and from that point the slate had to be wiped clean. I just couldn't concern myself with anything that may have happened before, even in the recent past at Leeds. All that rubbish deserved only one fate. It had to be dumped into the nearest dustbin and forgotten. And that's where it has stayed as far as I'm concerned from that day to this.

It was always my committed belief that this was the club to suit Cantona perfectly. Some players, many with respected and established reputations, are cowed and broken by the size and expectations of the place. Not Eric. He swaggered in, stuck his chest out, raised his head and surveyed everything as though he were asking: "I'm Cantona, how big are you? Are you big enough for me?" The question, I've got to say, is usually posed the other way round. I knew at that precise moment I could banish all my fears about him overnight.

Trying to sort the rubbish from reality is always a pointless exercise, in examining the great public myth of Cantona. The only wise course was not to be side-tracked. I just had to forget the worry about any outside distractions or influences and merely accept what Eric did on the field. Nothing else should be of concern to me or the club as long as his performance lived up to expectations. End of message. It was a policy of *laissez-faire*. Or to put it another way: there are certain rigid disciplinary codes that apply to everybody at United, but I have never purposely, or separately, asked Eric to stick to our rules. Everyone on the playing staff accepts there must be a recognised and acceptable level of behaviour and Eric has never stepped out of line.

Okay, he has been late for training a couple of times because of motorway hold-ups on the way from his Leeds home. He still lives there because his wife has a very good job at the university. The M62 bottle-neck has trapped him now and again so in the bleakest winter months he spends most of the week holed up in a Manchester hotel. Other than that, no problem. There are quite definitely no special privileges to keep him quiet.

Eric takes the stage

Relations are, appropriately, very much something of an *entente cordiale*. We must judge him by his performances and that's all. Anything else might be just a load of old cobblers. You could view it in the context of the condemned prisoner never being granted another chance. Where is the fairness and justice in that? You must be above that kind of thing. Eric has always been very fair with United; we must be absolutely fair with him. And long may it last. In my opinion - okay, I accept I'm biased - he was born to play for United.

When he walks into a room, or on to a football pitch anywhere you care to name, he has a presence about him. All eyes swivel in his direction. In the football business we are all actors. The pitch is the great stage for every one of us and some footballers want to be Douglas Fairbanks, Jr., if you remember him, all dashing and cavalier. Others, I'm afraid, see themselves as King Kong. We all recognise Eric's role. He is the true theatrical performer. The more important the performance, the more he is inspired by it. That proud chin juts out and and his manner seems to suggest: "Look how great I am, give me the ball. That's what I'm here for."

With Eric's arrival, some people maintained that the combination of my strong-minded management approach and his oddball streak amounted to an explosion waiting to happen. One little spark and the mushroom cloud would be seen rising above Old Trafford. I merely cautioned them when they mentioned his legendary temper: "Just wait until he sees mine - he hasn't seen anything yet."

Since that day we haven't had any bother, and I don't expect any either. Maybe it's got something to do with all those historic Celtic and Gallic alliances we have had down the centuries. Two nationalities with similar temperaments. More likely there is another fundamental reason: I only lose my temper for the right reasons. If a player is not reaching for a standard of performance which I know is within his capabilities, then I'm certainly likely to erupt. I wouldn't pull back from that reaction just because it might trigger something in a volatile personality like Cantona. But, so far, it's not been necessary because he has never slipped from his own demands for perfection - or the nearest he can get to it.

There are only two or three players in my whole life with whom I have never needed to lose my temper. Eric is one of them. The other two are Bryan Robson and Willie Miller. They reflect my image of life in general and football in particular. They mirror my desires and beliefs on how exactly the game should be played. They care very deeply

Cantona - "the true theatrical performer"

about not making mistakes. It is carelessness above all that drives me mad. There is no excuse for complacency and sloppiness on a football field, in training or when the chips are down. It's the antithesis of what I am - whatever your vocation, you must, above all, show care for the work you do.

When finely tuned players like Cantona or Giggs attempt something difficult in the last third, producing a magic touch in the desire to create a winning goal, and it goes slightly wrong, no problem. That's not carelessness, but a footballer taking risks with his craft. I admire and applaud that kind of attacking nerve and audacity. In my camp, that is never going to be criticised. It is the touch of genius that I knew Eric possessed. And I fully appreciated it could be the long lost key in turning the championship lock.

Miracle worker

He contributes so much to a game. He scores goals, creates goals and dreams up little miracles that are simply beyond the technical scope and imagination of most people. His vision and touch around the box sometimes stretch even my belief. He is just velvet - the way he can float balls, with precisely the right weight and angle, is an art form. The kind of moves he often attempts require absolute to-the-millimetre precision if they are not to go disastrously wrong. The goal in the Charity Shield was a classic. Inching back off the defender, caressing the ball on his boot and nursing it tenderly into the box for Mark Hughes. Wonderful to watch. So much quality and care encompassed in a split-second of football.

It was symbolic really. Because that's what motivates Cantona whenever he ties on his boots. In training, every pass has got to be on the button. He is a perfectionist and like so many Europeans his work-outs last longer than most. He asks for a couple of apprentices to stay out with him when the normal session has finished. He occupies himself for another half-hour or so polishing his already formidable array of skills. If one trick he attempts is slightly wrong, a scowl clouds his face and he gets very angry and loudly curses himself. There is an almost limitless professionalism and a fierce pride about his work.

At Coventry last season, he played with a fractured hand and the protection of little more than heavy strapping. He was clearly in pain out there. With 55 minutes on the watch, considering his injury and the fact that he had played just 72 hours earlier, I decided to take him off. I wanted to consolidate with the winning post coming into view. Big Eric didn't sympathise with or appreciate the substitution one little bit. He stalked off as though I had publicly insulted his ability. It was quite clearly an occasion where his football pride had been temporarily threatened.

Cantona - "the catalyst... a star who always shines brightly"

His mentor and close confidante is the great Michel Platini. He was a footballer of perfection and pride as well. Maybe he saw a football soul brother in Eric. Whatever it was, he promoted him strongly for the French national side and was convinced Cantona would benefit from broadening his game in Britain. Already, though, he had no doubts that he was seeing a player of genuine world-class stature. Once you have worked with him for a very short period, you would have to be blind not to see that as well. The entire United management and all the players swiftly accepted the fact. The proof of the pudding wasn't slow to materialise. We knew we had somebody special to help us be champions within a fortnight.

Cantona was the catalyst. I see the emergence of United as a major force underpinned by a huge team effort and dressing-room camaraderie. Nobody is the type to let a team-mate down. But there is another factor, too, and that's the romance and legend of this club. There is an unwritten obligation to the massive support, and the football culture of the whole institution, that you also have individuals with the showbiz streak of the great entertainers. So it's been of great satisfaction for me to see this championship side be so successful with that dual purpose in life. They play as a team in the fullest sense, but they also have the great stars like Cantona, Giggs, Hughes and Ince. Stars who are always allowed to shine brightly.

Part of the team

They light up the crowd with their individuality, but it never dims the overall performance of the team. That's what I like about our set-up, because you have to be extremely careful when you have so many individuals. The alarming danger is that each might be tempted to try that one trick too many to outdo the rest. Then it's chaos and the power of the team ethic just evaporates. You finish, in effect, with no team at all. To emphasise the point I keep reminding my players of the great Ruud Gullit. He can play - can he play! - but he never forgets the team as a whole. And that's the extra dimension of a player at the very pinnacle of his profession.

The United quartet I have mentioned don't shy away from hard work, either, even though they are equipped with special talents. Consequently we are a much better side that many with an all-star line-up. Because - and nobody appreciates the asset more than me - to emerge on top in the winning game it often takes the outstanding individual to get you there. Just the sight of Cantona in a red shirt was enough for the rest. It transformed them, galvanised them, and the goals began flowing again. The other players watched him in training and, from the day he arrived, you could see they were bowled over with his skill. I have watched as they have echoed the terrace chant: "Ooh, aah, Cantona - I say ooh-aah Cantona" when he pulled off something special in training. A big grin always floods Eric's face. Only Les Sealey is snarling when he has been sent hurtling the wrong way.

Eric has put a smile or two on my face as well and loaded up the memory banks with flashes of genius that will stay with me for years. I'll never forget some of the moments when Eric was able to turn the title towards its resting place in our boardroom. His goal against Middlesbrough when he juggled and shimmied the centre-half into a heap. I'll spare the lad's identity because by the time Cantona left him he must have had twisted blood! The first strike was

Ice-cool genius

blocked, but he picked up the bits and slammed in the rebound. Sensational stuff. The runaway dribble at Norwich in the last month, gliding through like one of those Stealth bombers, was just as exciting.

And then there was, of course, the night he wrecked the Palace. We knew Villa were going down the pan 3-0 at Blackburn. With twenty minutes left I brought Robson on for an expert shoring up operation to make sure nothing silly happened. Eric had other ideas. He delivered two passes, one for Hughes and the other for Ince which they both put away with clinical simplicity, and the execution in both cases was a superb combination of balance and touch. At that crucial stage championship nerves were a little frayed and the action was frenzied. But Cantona was still able to demonstrate that vital element of composure and accuracy. To be ice-cool in the heat of a very significant moment. Right then, he distinguished himself as being in a special league among players in British football.

Maybe that example captures the whole essence of Cantona. We all expect him to be different, and he has been exactly that - but only on the pitch. It's only that reputation, collected on his travels and not at United, that makes him stand alone. Maybe we are showing too much prejudice and being a little unfair to him. I've got to accept it doesn't seem to register with him all the same. Not on the outside anyway. All the media business about his wandering spirit and rebelliousness appears to slide off his back. In some instances I suspect he tries to exploit it and slyly take the mickey when they trail him around asking their questions.

Just recently I saw one Cantona interview in which his spectacular revelation was that next on the agenda for him was a particular wish to play in the GM Vauxhall Conference. No disrespect to the footballers down there, but do me a favour! It may simply be Eric's sense of humour. My reaction when this sort of thing drifts out is to treat it with a large pinch of garlic salt. As long as he is doing his training and playing on a Saturday, nothing else really matters. The prime concern is that Eric continues to influence our club's fortunes into the mid-nineties at least. I don't see any reason why he shouldn't.

He can see our high expectations and we understand his. As I have admitted money is not the motive in his life. He is driven by other desires and it's a fact that if finance was the ultimate consideration he could earn far more elsewhere, even in England. But for Cantona the real currency is pride in performance and achievement with a team that responds to his talents. Plus, a stage like Old Trafford where the magnificence of his football has the perfect backdrop. Only Real Madrid, Barcelona, Juventus and AC Milan can offer something similar. To leave here would almost certainly be to take a downward step and Eric is hardly the type who stoops to conquer.

Investing for the future

Eric was signed by me after earlier initiatives were made for Hirst, of England and Wednesday. They failed but not for the want of money or effort. Hirst, though, and not Alan Shearer, was always my No. 1 priority after we slipped up in the title scramble with Leeds. I knew we must have more goal power, and Hirst could provide it, but Trevor Francis was dismissive when the move was made. Not much later I was surprised to hear that Hirst had signed a new contract. To be honest that news stopped us in our tracks in planning the next phase of United's as well as his development.

I had focused on the big Barnsley lad because he's such an explosive player. He has lightning pace, possesses a power shot and has the strength to take any punishment meted out against him. He also had experience in the environment of a much bigger club than Shearer, then of course at Southampton. Alan was only 21, with much to prove, and with him you were buying potential. I felt the other option was better for us at that time. But you don't always have control in the transfer market and, late in the race, we had to switch horses.

For most of the season before Shearer's exit for Blackburn, I had monitored his situation at The Dell and kept in touch with their manager, Ian Branfoot. He said he would keep me informed, but asked me to back off for a while because he believed Shearer was prepared to sign a new Southampton contract. Next, the word came rattling down the line, that Shearer was in talks with Blackburn Rovers. Like Roy Keane, he shook hands with Kenny Dalglish and then came down for a chat with us. He went back to sign at Ewood Park, but let me emphasise we always had second billing in that particular transfer. Let's just say we intended to keep faith with our own pay codes and leave it at that.

The matter ended there, but my pursuit of a striker didn't. With Hirst out of the equation I laid my hands on a Cambridge video of Dion Dublin. As I scanned through it, one thing struck me very forcibly. The amazing variety of different style of goals big Dion collected, probably more than I had seen from any other finisher. I was impressed. At a million I thought he was worth the investment and I still believe his time at United will come again. But he suffered a nasty leg injury, one that really worried us for a time, when the goal drought bit for a second time. So once again we looked to Hirst for salvation.

But from Sheffield, despite a £3.5 million offer, there came only angry words in return. We tried to keep the transfer negotiations out of the newspapers but Trevor Francis appeared to read something else into it. All I can say is that he has a perfect right to turn down offers for his players, but I equally have the right to make the offer in the first place. That's all we did.

Just a matter of a month later we spoke to Leeds, called the bank and sunk our money in a fabulous investment. Eric Cantona.

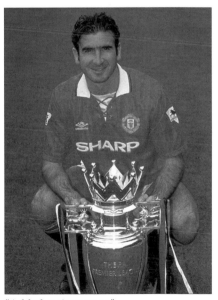

"A fabulous investment"

"Team selections, agonising decisions, dramatic incidents that turned matches our way, others that tortured me for days, wonderful performances and spectacular match-winning goals. I can remember in graphic detail every single moment."

CHAPTER EIGHT

The Title Race

What was it that Neil Armstrong, the American astronaut, said when he landed on the moon? "One small step for man," I think it was, "but one giant leap for mankind." Our championship conquest last season was hardly in the same league as lunar exploration, but I could certainly have borrowed good old Neil's pressure suit at times. And United's own flight of fantasy definitely demanded a lot of important steps, and one or two giant leaps as well, to make sure we landed in the right place when it mattered most in May.

I can remember in graphic detail every single one of them. All I need to do is flick a mental button, and the whole of the title race is just like viewing a video playback. Team selections, agonising decisions, dramatic incidents that turned matches our way, others that tortured me for days, wonderful performances and spectacular match-winning goals. They are locked in there for all time. Maybe you have them, too, but for the less privileged of our fans I reckon it's worth another trip down the championship's Memory Lane.

The first part of the journey was back across the Pennines to Bramall Lane, where Leeds United had beaten us to it approximately four months earlier. But that wasn't even preying on my mind any longer. Much more of a priority was making certain that we were in the right mental shape for the ninety minutes of bruising conflict with Sheffield United and the season ahead. It had to be a declaration of intent. We had to show the support that all the miseries of the past were forgotten and we were determined to go for the throat in the very first game. The date was August 15th, and Paul Ince launched himself into a crash-bang challenge that appeared to indicate he didn't care to see the sixteenth!

I wanted my players to prove we were alive and full of spirit, not demoralised or down in any way. But Incey almost killed himself in attempting to demonstrate my philosophy! Virtually from the kick-off he made a raging-bull charge for fully sixty yards, clattered their goalkeeper and ended up in a stunned heap. So he was carted off for treatment. Even worse was the immediate result. He had been detailed to take the near post at any of Sheffield's well rehearsed set-pieces. Of course he was missing when they took a long throw, we hadn't marked up properly and they scored. Terrific! Two minutes into the new season and we were behind with one of our best players

Paul Ince - "almost killing himself demonstrating my philosophy"

stretched out on the touchline. We should have had a penalty and didn't get it; they appealed for one later and did. By the time Mark Hughes scored it wasn't enough for us and we lost 2-1.

Defeat in the opening match was hardly part of the plans but, as always in football, there is another game round the corner to repair the broken dream almost instantly.

Four days later Everton came to Old Trafford. The briefing was simplicity itself - this game we must win. Unluckily for us, Neville Southall had other ideas. We set about the task with real application and drive, but he made two amazing first-half saves from Hughes. Just before half time we lost our discipline and Peter Beardsley sprang the trap. One down. Two more Everton breakaways in the next forty-five and we had been dumped to a 3-0 defeat. I looked at the scoreline and felt the world had come to an end. After losing the previous championship in dramatic circumstances, I didn't believe this was happening to me again.

Bottoms up

The papers thought it was their birthday. "Bottoms Up, Fergie!" screamed the morning's headlines, playing on the troubles of Sarah Ferguson, the Duchess of York, as well as my own. I quietly convinced myself we had performed to a decent level, but to win matches you needed an end product. We hadn't provided one and, consequently, had gone down twice. That aspect urgently had to be put right before we surrendered too much ground to the rest. Next on the home agenda, newly promoted Ipswich. We improved quite a bit and really deserved to win. Once again, though, we squandered chances. They scored with a scrappy goal and Irwin delivered a smashing equaliser, but the whistle called the draw at 1-1. In the post-match TV interview I declared that the only option now was for us to bare-knuckle it for results. Fight and scrap for a point here and there to get back among the early front-runners.

Beginning to win

Off we headed for the Monday night game on the box at Southampton. A tight, cramped little ground that's never easy to make an impression in. But we just had to win to avert a looming disaster. I gave our new signing Dion Dublin the nod for his first full game and he presented his own reward with a last minute winner. That 1-0 result, and the way it was achieved, typified so many of the performances that secured our ultimate success. The goal came late, like about fifteen others that were struck in various fixtures throughout the season in the final ten minutes of the match. For me, there is absolute proof in those statistics that we have a United team of real substance, a unit of resilience and determination. They are qualities you must have in abundance to survive a marathon. And it also indicated the resolve and nerve of the side. The first three-pointer felt good, too, as we left Arsenal at the bottom to take all the stick on their own, unfairly in my mind. Suddenly we were up and running for five straight wins.

Dion Dublin- "real resilience and determination"

Brian Clough's Forest were a long-prized victim. They effectively did more damage to us in the previous championship than any other single bunch of players in the country. They had completed the League double over us and that hurt. I sensed the determination among the team; they wanted revenge. At the time Forest had started to flounder after beating Liverpool on the first Sunday of the season. Their defence was in disarray in dealing with the new pass back rule and I emphasised that point in the team talk. Dublin and Ince underlined the fact by blocking umpteen attempted clearances by their 'keeper, Mark Crossley. By half time we should have been three or four in front. Instead there was a typical blockbuster from Sparky in the bottom corner after Ince worked the space. My son Darren carried out a superb containment plan on Roy Keane and Ryan Giggs sorted everything with a second half header. Comfortable win: 2-0.

Steve Coppell, always a formidable opponent with his tenacious, hard-working teams, arrived next with Crystal Palace. We didn't, admittedly, play very well but we had to cope with their sweeper system and that in itself was a crucial lesson when we made the return trip to Selhurst Park in April. I suspected they would stick by the same strategy on the night we turned the title our way in south London - and they did exactly that. Mark Hughes's goal guaranteed a gutsy, if unspectacular, 1-0 win that was tainted by a very serious injury to new boy Dublin. He was caught by an Eric Young tackle from behind and his leg was in such a mess we were genuinely worried about his playing career for a while. But I think Dion was just unlucky, caught out in the wrong place on a greasy surface, because my own view is that there was nothing malicious or naughty about the challenge.

Leeds posed us problems of a different kind four days later. They swarmed all over the place in the early exchanges and almost collected a goal or two. But, once we established our own presence, one factor was rapidly obvious: their defensive structure wasn't too sound. With only a fraction more good fortune Hughes would have had four goals chalked against his name. John Lukic rescued his team-mates with a whole series of tremendous saves. He wasn't able to repel Steve Bruce or Andrei Kanchelskis, though, and we ended up with a 2-0 win. I knew immediately, with home success against Palace and Leeds secured, my team was really back on the road.

This planet didn't seem such a bad place after all. The head scratchers wondered what made all the difference to us. The answer is elementary - simply: confidence. It's the ultimate factor in football. Players are transformed and reinforced by it. They all want to be out there playing in the side. All of a sudden the injury niggles are no longer there. Nor the "I'm not sure if I can make this one, boss" type of comments. The doubts have vanished and it's Everton on the hit list. The trip to Merseyside, and the small matter of some unresolved business after the way they whipped us a month earlier, couldn't have been timed better.

Andrei Kanchelskis - "unstoppable"

The performance was solid, Choccy McClair claimed his first goal of the season while Bruce added to his collection, and we were spurred on by the knowledge that we had won well at Goodison Park. Howard Kendall thought so, too. He emerged from their dressing-room with the freely given opinion that he considered he had just seen the future League champions. Now that's the kind of confidence vote in football that I wouldn't mind listening to every day of the week because it had the extra credibility of coming from a man who knew all about feeling champion. Howard had been top of the pile twice himself in the eighties. It certainly had a beneficial influence on United's whole squad in the long-term, even if the immediate effect didn't materialise in the goal-less draw with Torpedo Moscow in the UEFA Cup.

Worrying signs first appeared at Tottenham on September 19th. I ringed that day in my championship diary, because that's where the carelessness and complacency that can cost titles really started. We should all remember the fabulous individual goal from Giggs which I described a couple of chapters ago. But we blew away incredible chances just after half time, lost concentration and Spurs nicked the equaliser on the break. Two points thrown away at 1-1. It was the first goal we had lost in seven matches and it stopped up our rhythm and flow.

QPR, the team that had trampled us the previous New Year with their

Alarm bells ringing

impressive pass-and-move approach, didn't help much either. They stifled us and limited us to one half chance when Hughes tried a cheeky back heel and the big 'keeper Jan Stejskal read it at the post. We piled a lot into their box without threatening any havoc. More heartache for me and 0-0 in the record books. So

the casualness of White Hart Lane caught up with us, aggravated by the creative failure against the visiting Russians and our championship momentum was effectively sabotaged. I was concerned that old problems had again seeped into the system to threaten our ambitions. In passing, there was the brief interruption of Brighton in the Coca Cola Cup, a Danny Wallace goal and a 1-1 draw even though we should have cruised it by three or four. From a position of strength when we had climbed to the top three in the Premier League, it was a dangerous slide down the

Ryan Giggs on his way to "a fabulous individual goal"

hill. We allowed sheer carelessness to undermine all our previous efforts. Next was Moscow and, chillingly, no goals and a penalty shoot-out going against us after we should have scored another sackful. In my experience that is what so often happens with United. We can be inspired to surge forward on a sensational run of results or, just as dramatically, be dragged back by a terrible sequence of failure.

Back on form

At Middlesbrough we again failed to free ourselves from the shackles. We dominated the game on a paddy-field of a surface at Ayresome Park but had to be content with a Steve Bruce penalty. They scored late and again I held my private inquest with one question at the forefront: "How the hell did we not win that match?" Even their manager Lennie Lawrence, delighted at 1-1, reckoned he wouldn't have been too distraught if Middlesbrough had lost it by three or four considering the volume of chances we created. For them it was a miracle result. I counted up the results, an alarming six draws on the trot, and in three of them we hadn't scored a goal. After an inspiring early acceleration to catch up with the leadership pack we had just hit the wall. My mind was clear - I wasn't going to tolerate such meagre rewards for very much longer. Once again I started sifting through the list of strikers for possible targets, with David Hirst on top of the pile. I knew I had to dabble in the market once more, or we could lose the initiative.

When Liverpool checked in at Old Trafford we were lucky to escape with a 2-2 result. They swept efficiently into the lead and - no arguments whatsoever, they deserved to be in front. I could detect too many jaded, tired-out players in my team after the midweek internationals. Nine of the top men had been away playing for their countries. It showed. Ince, so often the man with the whip hand in the midfield, was just exhausted. He was clearly drained from his contribution to the England cause at Wembley. That was the invitation for Liverpool and they took control and overran us in that area of the park. Two great efforts from

Hughes in the final ten minutes saved us; one was an absolute peach when he noticed Bruce Grobbelaar off the line and found him out with a classic chipped goal. Okay, we put a few attacks together in the last third of the game, but certainly luck was on our side in prising a point we hadn't really deserved.

Kenny Dalglish enjoyed some luck of his own a week later at Ewood Park. His Blackburn team were grateful for so many narrow escapes, but it was still 0-0. Bad news. Brucie had a header taken off the line and Clayton Blackmore, slotted in to the right-hand midfield job instead of Kanchelskis, could easily have had a hat-trick. If we hadn't played so well another chunk of confidence might have been chiselled away. The goal drought of the previous season left us all feeling pretty low, but this was different. Reasonably good performance levels proved to be my consolation at that stage.

Down to Villa on the Wednesday for the Coca Cola Cup and I don't think we have ever created more chances in a game without finding the net than in that particular tie. It was agonising to watch. Some of our football was brilliant but Dean Saunders made us suffer with the lone winner from a corner. Yet another defeat to damage the self-belief of the United strikers. All we needed at that stage was the sight of Wimbledon's arrival at the weekend. Out of the Cup, unable to score a goal or two, not in 100% shape, and then the Wombles had to knock on our door. Just wonderful. Vinnie Jones scored the only goal from a Terry Gibson free kick. One more example of a former player who had returned to haunt me. Wimbledon were full of it. They danced in the corridor to the usual ghetto-blaster. The usual circus behaviour from them. It was more like a ruddy disco than a football ground. It didn't, rest assured, go down too well with the United lads.

Shopping time

But that result triggered the inevitable for me. I needed to exercise serious thought in buying a new front player. The thread of failure from the previous season when we slumped into a deep decline after Christmas was there for all of us to see. I knew I couldn't possibly allow that to happen again. That course of action was galvanised by the League return to Villa Park. We ended up being well beaten even though the record books show only a one-goal defeat. Without a magnificent performance from Peter Schmeichel it would have been a good few more. He pulled down a power header from Paul McGrath and was also brave in flying at the feet of Saunders and Dalian Atkinson with saves that prevented a rout.

But the one significant move from that game, as bad as the overall performance proved, was the re-emergence of Lee Sharpe and Bryan Robson. I played them for long-term benefit and not short-term results. I accepted after two or three A-team workouts that they weren't in competitive shape, but I believed it was the right time to thrust them into the top quality games they needed to progress. We had to have an injection of new belief and Robson is always going to provide that. His big name presence is enough and invariably he gives an extra dimension to United when he takes the field. But the come-back pair were the only silver lining amid the growing clouds of despair. Relief came in the shape of a two week break while the World Cup dates were fitted in and it gave me the opportunity to play both Robson and Sharpe in friendlies at Chester and Aberdeen. By the time Oldham Athletic loomed on the horizon they were so much more of a powerful option, fit and ready for action.

The game against Latics was almost akin to being transported to a different planet. At half time we were three up with McClair able to celebrate a double and the other one down to Hughes. The only reason we took our foot off the pedal was because Sharpe and Robson tired later in the game. But, overall, we were refreshed and the cobwebs of gloom had been blown away. The wagon train was on a roll again and, it seemed, headed in the right direction after a few too many detours for my liking. That week also marked the arrival of Cantona and what I hoped would be a new view from the terraces. I considered that the traumas of the previous weeks, and then the transformation in our game, taught the fans that patience was the critical asset if we were ever to be champions again.

New signing Cantona at the Arsenal match

Big Eric, a signing forced on us to some degree by the September injury to Dublin who would have granted me a much needed option, was unable to play at Arsenal. The registration had been delayed slightly so he was perched up in the Highbury stand. But even from that vantage point I am still convinced he was our inspiration against Arsenal. It was more than a suspicion in my mind that the other players swore to themselves that day: "Cantona is a big threat now, but I'm not going to be the one left out for him." Robbo, a ship-steadier if ever there was one, gave the whole team a sense of purpose. Giggs clearly accepted that he could do a job for us on the right-hand side. That switch had troubled him for a while. The formula worked, anyway, because it turned into a brilliant, collective performance with Hughes again snatching the winner when Arsenal were relieved not to have been buried. I knew then we were back as a real championship force.

Slipping up

From November 21, in fact, to the end of the whole campaign we lost only two matches - at Oldham and Ipswich, and Cantona missed only the one at Boundary Park. Surely no other statistic was ever more important in the winning of the title. Next we beat Manchester City 2-1 at home and Eric made his first bow. I brought him on as a half-time sub for Giggs and he made an immediate impression. He transformed the game and the crowd loved him. Ince scored with a great strike from outside the box and Hughes wrapped it up with a half-volley. That victory put us in the right frame of mind for a confrontation six days later that we just had to win.

Norwich arrived in town. They were on top of the Premier League, nine points clear of ourselves and the chasing pack. Somebody had to peg them back before they escaped and ran clear. It was vital we stopped their gallop and we did. Hughes was the predator when one of their defenders failed to control a Sharpe cross properly. He allowed the ball to run free and Sparky pounced and put it away to the right of Bryan Gunn. Norwich were positive, though, and played some bright football but the result was ours. The gap had been narrowed to six points between us.

The next crucial move was mine at Chelsea and, hands held up in apology, I made a mistake. I picked the wrong team. They were going well at the time and I was very concerned about the damage their midfield three might inflict on us. I looked at the pitch, too, and it was decidedly dodgy. I made up my mind it was a day for grafters and I put Mike Phelan on to do watch-dog duty on Andy Townsend. But it was only when I revised the master plan and restored Andrei Kanchelskis to the attack that we really started to play. And, in the end, Eric secured us a precious away point with his first goal for United. With plenty of French dressing, too. He turned majestically on Phelan's lay-off from a Sharpe cross and placed it with a flourish in the far corner. That demonstrated his capacity for fashioning important goals.

In return Cantona was shown the full magnetism and drama of the British game at Sheffield Wednesday. The 3-3 result on Boxing Day was the kind of spectacle that has fans two decades later letting everybody in earshot know they were there. Aye, it was that good. Even today I can only hazard a guess at what the score should have been. In running the video through what I do know is that we made eighteen good chances and should have scored from sixteen of them. Honestly. Wednesday got two in five minutes and we should have had five *Bonjour, Eric* ourselves in the first quarter-hour. It was a wonderful, incredible game and Trevor Francis's team might have had six or seven goals on their credit sheet. Instead, they went three in front and that meant it had to be a gung-ho exercise for United. I don't think there is any team around that is better at that kind of football.

We got back to 3-2, both from McClair headers. For the first one Sharpe's cross was half-cleared from the box but Paul Parker passed it back to Sharpe, who whipped it in to the far post where Choccy was waiting. Sharpe linked with Ince for the next one and again McClair kept his nerve to put us back in the contest. The equaliser was a nightmare really - at least for me, trapped helpless on the bench. We had ten players camped out in their half and I swear to this day it might just have been eleven with Schmeichel on an overlap. He's certainly mad enough to attempt it. Anyway, Pallister shaped a ball through for Sharpe. Cantona, amazingly for him, had a

Cantona - toe-pokes the equaliser against Wednesday

mis-kick on the cross but was quick enough to toe-poke the loose ball over the line before Chris Woods was able to stop him. It was all square but we could have had two more in the last four minutes when Sharpe missed out on a great day.

Over the last few years I have shared, in the management sense, in a few United matches of that level of high drama and calibre. After them you sit in the boot room feeling absolutely whacked - and you haven't even kicked a ball. But it's always a fabulous feeling to have been involved in the kind of football entertainment on which United's image and reputation has been created.

Into our stride
The next fixture against Coventry was of a similar vintage and contained some of the finest attacking play I have ever seen from a team of mine. It underlined perfectly the period of transformation in the way United could perform. The goal-less deadlocks were banished to the past and, suddenly, Giggs was flying, Sharpe looked as though he had never been away, and there was swagger about everybody.

Coventry were clouted by five goals, all from different scorers with one central theme: Cantona had a focal part in every single one. Big Eric claimed his own along with Denis Irwin, Sharpe, Hughes and Giggs. At the time Coventry had just demolished Liverpool 5-1 and also clattered Villa 3-0 and their manager, Bobby Gould, was magnanimous in defeat. He recognised publicly that his players had been taken apart by a team as good as any in Europe. It was the New Year and we were back on top - fired by championship resolution.

Memories of what had happened at the same time a year earlier did filter back into my mind. Our best form then had been in the month of December. The six goal walloping we had inflicted on Oldham on their ground, the two Cup victories, plus a League draw with Leeds United at Elland Road, were the main

features in that particular script. So I wondered quietly what was going to develop this time around. A little apprehension, a private worry or two, but I was also far more confident, reassured, about the team. I felt they were stronger and better equipped for the task ahead in '93. We had been down that road once and weren't scared of the route any more. There were no bogeymen waiting for us this time. Or if there were we knew we could deal with them. Experience is one of football's greatest allies.

The first round of the FA Cup fixed us up with close neighbours Bury at home. I

Keith Gillespie scores for United on his debut

blooded young Keith Gillespie and he blessed his debut with a goal. Mike Phelan also notched his first for us at Old Trafford and we didn't have too much bother. The goals seemed to be flooding back in another outstanding show with Spurs. We swept them aside 4-1 and had four different scorers on the sheet with Paul Parker claiming his first United goal against the club he supported as a boy. Spurs' consolation was tucked away in the last minute and the margin of victory was more comprehensive than it appeared. Terry Venables missed the match on some personal matter but he rang me a few days later and said: "I understand your boys annihilated us - thank heavens I wasn't there to witness it." Nice call, Tel, and one that carried an encouraging message for us.

But, sadly, we suffered a problem with Cantona. He collected a hamstring strain and, because we didn't know him too well then and possessed few details of his injury record, I decided to show caution. We tried to impress on Eric that if he gambled he could be out of football for five or six weeks. He wanted to play, though, and at QPR there was some explaining to do before I left him out. It was a Monday night TV game and the omens were healthy. All season long we didn't lose a single one of them. And the scoreline, amazingly, was always 3-1!

With Eric counted out, I opted for Hughes and Giggs down the middle. It was a fantastic performance that was largely overshadowed by over-physical methods that you don't normally associate with Rangers. It started with an uncharacteristic lunge by Andy Sinton on Paul Parker. The challenge was nasty but totally unexpected from Sinton, particularly as the victim was one of his best friends in the game. Their centre-half, Alan McDonald, also went through Sparky from behind with a terrible tackle and he ended up being carried of. Hughes needed ten stitches in a badly gashed calf. It was suggested later that there might have been bad feeling because of McDonald's sending off after another incident with Sparky in 1989. But my recollection of that was that McDonald received the red card for an elbow offence that later brought a club fine. So Hughes was the innocent party and I would hate to think the big defender had held a grudge for four years.

Dirty work

Rangers' behaviour was most unlike a Gerry Francis side. They normally like to get the ball down and play. The year before they slaughtered us at Old Trafford and I deliberately looked out for Gerry to congratulate him on the performance. My conviction is that among the younger breed of managers in the game he is destined for the very top. The uglier side of Rangers demonstrated on that January night was nothing more than a one-off as far as I was concerned. My only grievance was that the press ignored an excellent display from the United players in their eagerness to cook up rumours of ill feeling. I also think the referee John Martin, who always likes the game to flow, might just have called it wrong on the

Mark Hughes - "the innocent party" after a tackle from QPR's Alan McDonald

night. But Ince scored a cracker with an athletic overhead that he claimed was intentional; I didn't believe him for a moment! The other two were served up by Giggs and Kanchelskis.

Our Welsh wonder stole another headline or two in the next Cup tie with Brighton at home. He collected the United winner near the end with a display of his ever-improving technique at free kicks. It was probably the first public demonstration of how lethal Ryan is in such a situation. He and Denis Irwin have made a great deal of progress with the goal-scoring set-piece because they practice for hours on a special wall we have at the training ground. Not quite the famous dustbin routine, but a marvellous coil-back barrier that is just like facing the real thing in a game. The lads swear by it.

Cloughie's Forest were next on the title hit list. Ince swept in the breakthrough goal helped by a defensive deflection and then Hughes lifted the terraces with one of his special strikes. Cantona supplied the pass that Sparky dispatched with a stunning half-volley. To be fair, we should have been five in front in the first twenty minutes before Forest rallied. Their reward in that period could have been a couple of goals at least. In the end we proved the stronger team, though. A sound performance, a good result and we were back on top of the League. The date was January 27th.

Dawn of a new United

The bags were packed and off we went to Ipswich. Down at Portman Road we suffered our first defeat since the arrival of Cantona. But I sniffed all the ingredients of a shock that day. Their pitch was in a bit of a state and, as they did for much of last season, Ipswich operated a man-marking system. They took the lead from an extremely rare mistake by Schmeichel. In this era of the back pass law it was the kind that any manager dreads. He came out for a long ball, swung a leg and missed it completely: 1-0. I figured the writing was on the wall as soon as it went in. Their second beat us via a ricochet and when McClair grabbed one back late on, it was created from sheer endeavour more than anything else. But you never survive any title campaign without suffering a setback or two and, on reflection, that result was an important reminder for the team. Everything had been running sweetly smooth and the lesson was there of how it can all turn sour in seconds.

I was far from discouraged and still felt that a new United was under impressive development at that time. A side constructed around endurance and resilience as well as skill, a combination of various qualities boasted by all the best teams. They increasingly showed that capacity to turn a game and win it in the last ten or fifteen minutes with the odds stacked heavily against them. Perseverance got us there against Sheffield United, for instance. We were a goal behind with time fast running out when McClair nicked the equaliser from Cantona's header. The Frenchman turned up with the winner just three minutes before the finish. But, unfortunately for us, Eric was on international duty when we headed for Bramall Lane with the opportunity for Dave Bassett's team to gain revenge.

In the FA Cup the following week, once Giggs scored we looked as though we would coast through the fifth round tie, but the eventual verdict had to be that we simply defended very badly. Everybody in the game appreciates that Bassett's teams are superb with set-pieces and we just didn't handle them well. They scored from two inside a minute and we ended up in trouble. Okay, in my opinion, we might have been given three penalties instead of the one that Steve Bruce missed in the last minute of the game. The order should have been for the skipper to re-take it because his concentration was affected as Sheffield's Bryan Gayle was allowed to stand just a yard from the referee, Mike Reed from Birmingham. We ended up calling the ref all the names under the sun but, with hindsight, it was arguably the greatest favour he could grant us. Out of the Coca Cola, Europe and then the FA Cup, allowing us to focus on just one objective.

The resilient nature of the players was underlined in the next fixture at home to Southampton. With nine minutes of the match remaining we were a goal down and praying for salvation from somewhere. From anywhere. Giggs had the answer with two exciting, match-winning goals in a minute. There was a desperate need for real determination after the Cup disaster. This victory was further evidence that I now had a team that could take a kick in the teeth and still clamber off the floor and have another go. Boro', the next opponents, were still flat out on the deck when we beat them.

Cantona helping United towards a victory against Middlesbrough

Without key personnel, they were forced to patch things up at the back with emergency solutions, and it showed. Their form was also on the wane and we should have won by a landslide. Giggs, Ince and Cantona made the score-sheet that day, but I felt sorry for the Boro' manager, Lennie Lawrence. At all his clubs he has proved himself a very efficient operator, but he was up against the wall for our match. The relegation curse appeared to be gripping his club and dragging them down.

That was also the point where we approached a month of destiny. In front of us was one hell of a fixture schedule with Liverpool, Oldham and Manchester City away and great rivals Villa and Arsenal at Old Trafford. I felt that if we survived that little lot and were still no more than two points adrift of the leaders, we would be in with a real shout. Up to Anfield and a win that appeared a lot easier on the video later than it ever did during the live ninety minutes. Liverpool kicked off with that typical surge of power and it needed Schmeichel's massive presence to deny them. We had no Cantona; he was suspended. But from the moment Giggs started to run at their back four we were in charge. Hughes put us ahead but Rush caught us unawares with one of those spectacular spin-turns and finishes. Midway through the second half McClair delivered the winner. The victory was a landmark for me because I hadn't won there since Norman Whiteside did the business back in my first season. More important still, it meant we were ahead of our points target for the month.

I fully understood and never underestimated the threat posed by Oldham in the following match. They were locked in a fight for their lives in the Premier League and they dug deep into their souls against us. We surrendered a sloppy goal from a corner, when our marking was all over the place, and apart from a

McClair strike against the bar we had not created much attacking mischief. The United players knew it as well, although Joe Royle's players had certainly earned the three points.

Paving the way

In the judgement of many our next game against Villa was the championship decider. What is indisputable is that it shaped up into a very special sporting contest. It was ninety minutes of fully committed football, with not a nasty tackle or mouthy confrontation between any players, and it measured up to a tremendous advert for the modern game. Ron Atkinson stressed afterwards that Villa's defence was brilliant. Their goalkeeper Mark Bosnich, a former United player, was outstanding with at least six marvellous stops. But he wasn't able to prevent a Hughes equaliser, after Steve Staunton had silenced the stadium. What a hit it was from him - I can still hear the sound of his shot when it drummed against the stanchion. But there was extra comfort for me in the belief that we had proved ourselves the better team even if Villa had seized a point at a crucial moment for them.

The month that mattered hadn't damaged us too much. We embroiled ourselves in a typical derby game with City at Maine Road. I'll never forget the stonewall penalty we should have been given in the second half when Hughes was hauled back by Keith Curle. Mind you, we only had two penalties all year - probably fewer than any champions in history - so we were used to it. Nobody could accuse us of receiving a helping hand from the referee on our way to the top. A terrific header from Cantona rescued the game for us at 1-1 after Niall Quinn popped one in. The big City striker enjoyed himself against Schmeichel last year with goals in both derby matches and another in the World Cup tie against Denmark.

Ryan Giggs "embroiled in a typical derby at Maine Road"

The last game in March was Arsenal at home. The Force was with us that night and we carried a fair amount of luck in surviving goal chances they created. Paul Merson, I remember, shuddered the bar in the last five minutes. Secretly, I always felt a win then and the title was effectively ours. I always fancied that Norwich would beat Villa, who hadn't won at Carrow Road in 12 years, and I was proved right. As we slugged it out with Arsenal we knew the result down there, too, but no matter how much encouragement was provided by our crowd the winning result was beyond us. Even Robbo in the last fifteen minutes couldn't alter the course of a goal-less deadlock. Still, we were within two points of Villa and I knew in my heart we were definitely favourites in the race. Our programme was by comparison slightly easier.

Was the TV game at Norwich going to prove another omen? They had played one game more and were leaders of a three team pack at the time. Hughes was suspended and I decided to stick with the 4-4-2 formation with Kanchelskis and Sharpe as the wide boys with Giggs floating through the middle alongside Cantona. Therefore, no Robson. We scored three fantastic goals in ten minutes through Giggs, Cantona and Kanchelskis. Some of the first half football must match anything in the history of the club. It could have been six even though Norwich belly-ached about two of the goals being offside. The TV replays proved that justice was on our side and it was a tell-tale result for us after Villa's failure on the same ground the week before. It must have left Ron's team thinking they were up against it.

Never too late

But, for many people, the championship crunch was surely the amazing switch-game with Sheffield Wednesday. I still have the vivid memory of thousands of United fans trooping out of Old Trafford when John Sheridan's penalty put them ahead. Their heads were lowered as they left and the support clearly couldn't take in what was happening to them. The reminders of the previous season were just too painful to accept. By that time the Villa lads must have been in the bath, hurt by their own home draw with Coventry but consoled by the knowledge that we looked like losing. Then Steve Bruce, with four minutes left of normal time, claimed the equaliser. Seven minutes into overtime he bagged another and it ended 2-1. A truly sensational result for us and we finished a point in front with just five games left to play. Our bench was full of crazy men and I must apologise for the behaviour of my assistant manager! But Villa weren't finished yet. They headed for Arsenal on the Monday, a game I believed they would lose, and won 1-0.

At the same time we were booked in at Highfield Road for the game with Coventry. The pitch was spongy, the performance dogged and no more. Cantona played with heavy strapping on a broken wrist, an injury collected in the epic struggle with Wednesday, but I replaced him with Robson in the

Denis Irwin scores during a dogged performance at Highfield Road

second half. I felt the need for added protection after Denis Irwin scored. The game finished with an element of controversy when Mick Quinn was sent off after a tussle with Schmeichel. But the referee later backtracked after watching a video which showed that he was big enough to think again. I applaud the use of TV replays to prove players innocent as well as guilty. But in that match Quinn was lucky not to be red carded for three terrible tackles.

The climax to that match was comfortable, but the next one with Chelsea was a stroll. Hughes whipped in the first as Dave Beasant was unluckily sent flying the wrong way by a deflection. An own goal just before half time and a third from

Hughesie cruising against Chelsea

Cantona just after wrapped up proceedings. I was able to rest Giggs and give Robson an extended run-out. All we had to do was wait for Sunday and the Villa game with Manchester City. I decided to impose my own television ban for the first time and watch a Western with Hendry Fonda on the other side. All went well until my wife Cathy told me City were in front. I couldn't resist the temptation and flicked the remote on to the match every minute or two. In the end I was out in the back garden pacing up and down. Villa eventually got back into it and won - and that's when I vowed I would never bother with their results again. All that mattered was my team and concentrating on winning the next three games and the League.

Cruising into history

The invitation to the Palace was of obvious importance. I suspected they would take us on with five at the back but my own plans received a jolt when Sharpe was sick-listed by a virus. The question revolved around a change of tactics in the use of Robson, but I decided to stick with the tried and trusted formula and played Kanchelskis wide on the right. The first half was just a slugging match, but the dramatic news filtered through from Blackburn that Villa had gone three down. I was out of the blocks from the directors' box to the dressing-room to pass on the information. In normal circumstances I would never do that, but I had an extraordinary situation on my hands. I knew we were in the clear then and simply stressed to the players that calmness was the only quality that mattered. Cantona showed how by setting up two great goals for Hughes and Ince. Two-nil - all over, really, with a four point lead and just two games left.

The rest, as they say, is history. Villa lost to Oldham on the Sunday, we collected the long-chased crown without kicking a ball, and finished the programme as though it were a carnival. Three-one against Blackburn with the plunder claimed by Ince, Giggs and Gary Pallister's first goal of the season. At Wimbledon six days later Ince was again on the sheet and Robson's strike meant that every one of our outfield players had a championship goal chalked against his name.

That was the icing on the cake, and the cake was a twenty-six tier dream come true that we were determined to have and to hold from that day forth.

*"Bryan reached for the stars
and they knew he was one of
the blessed"'*

CHAPTER NINE

Bryan & Lee

One dreaded word was whispered in my ear about Lee Sharpe and the reaction was instant and to be expected. Total panic. The alarming word, of course, was *meningitis* and it's the kind of medical definition that inevitably forces a shudder from all lay people. You think immediately of brain damage, even death, but always of a nightmare illness. So when we were told about young Lee's condition in the summer of '92, it was enough to spread a mood of despair and alarm throughout the club until we were told the truth: he wasn't going to die.

As a football manager, you learn to cope with most details of the job. In my time at the club I have handled decisions that ended the careers of Gary Bailey, a proven England international and a World Cup player when I arrived, and Remi Moses, another fantastic footballer. Billy Garton was also forced to quit through illness, while injury wiped out all the high expectations of younger players like Nicky Wood, John Bottomley and Tony Gill. They all presented tricky dilemmas that had to be handled with care and compassion. In dealing with the individual concerned, you must always make certain the enthusiasm and hopes of their team-mates aren't damaged at the same time. That aspect of management responsibility is learned along the way.

Sharpe panic

But nothing you have ever coped with, no matter how long in the tooth or experienced, can ever prepare you for the Sharpe situation. There is that unfathomable fear about meningitis and when Dr. Francis McHugh, the club's medical officer, called me at home with the report on Sharpe, I was stunned. And panicking. We all were. The worry was for Lee's whole future and in those first few seconds two questions ran through my head: "Hell, what do I say to the kid

Lee Sharpe - "From the depths of his deepest despair he climbed to the heights of being a champion."

about this?" and "How do I break this kind of news to his parents?" It was all so scary and my initial thought was focused on the widely held belief that this particular disease costs the lives of so many people. But the reassuring words of the Doc very swiftly swept my own fears aside.

The expert advice was that Lee, certainly in one respect, was fortunate. His problem was viral meningitis and not the frightening complaint that causes so much tragedy and sometimes even death. But the doctor also warned me that United must be reconciled to the fact that a very valuable player was certain to be out of football action for a very long time. The confident forecast suggested Lee would certainly recover, but he would not be able to do anything for at least three months. Still, it was another sickener for Sharpey. The year before he had missed countless games through groin and hernia problems that eventually took surgery to sort out.

He certainly was in need of bedside comfort and sympathy more than at any time in his life. Naturally, I went to see him with a message from the whole club. It was the very obvious reassurance that his particular problem was only temporary and wasn't the end for him. There was no question of that. We would stand by him and protect him during his recovery.

Stand by Lee

The first step was a rapidly arranged media briefing at which Dr. McHugh explained to the world the full details of Lee's illness. We intended to avoid any rumour mongering that, in fact, United had a footballer on their hands who was dying. He was far from ever being in that kind of danger, because his virus didn't affect the brain or threaten life. The other major step was to discover whether it might be contagious and affect other players in the squad. That wasn't a problem either, so it was just a matter of being patient.

Lee's problem was discovered when he returned from a summer holiday in Greece, where he might have contracted the virus, and started the pre-season physical build-up. He complained several times about blinding headaches, dizziness and also suffered from the occasional blackout. Hospital tests were the only answer. After a two-day check up, Lee was released to await the results. On the Old Trafford car park he collapsed again and was rushed back to the hospital. It happened to him two or three times before the medical bulletin delivered the verdict and I drove to see Lee's parents. I explained to them that his recovery and his United career were not in any danger and the specialist also offered his own very comforting words. After consulting the top men I never thought we had lost Sharpey for good, though I didn't expect him to play again for a full season.

Lee wasn't allowed near the place until we were absolutely sure the virus was cleared up. For fully three months we nursed Lee through it and stuck rigidly to the rehabilitation programme fixed by our medical advisers and the specialist in particular. Patience was the watchword for me. I was, admittedly, concerned about any long-term psychological effects on him as a player but that has proved groundless. And there was the issue of whether the illness might return in the future. I'm advised it won't.

The press played the game and allowed Lee to get back in shape without pestering him, except for one so-called newspaper. They trade on Sunday and claim to deal in sport, but they don't convince me and they certainly don't deserve a free plug in this book. Anyway, they banged on Lee's door without any helpful response and then attempted to slur his character with the inference that other factors were involved in Lee's illness. An example of the worst kind of scurrilous journalism, in fact.

By November, anyway, he was back in the first team. And that's where Lee, of all the players in the title squad, made the most dramatic move of his career without stepping outside our club. From the depths of his deepest despair he climbed to the heights of being a champion and also gained a recall for England. Incredible stuff, really. He has insisted since that from Christmas onwards he operated basically on pure adrenalin and didn't think he played too well. But that was never my view. Of course, there were the inevitable dips in performances when he was quiet and made little impact in games, but he still provided the crosses that carried us all to glory. I reckon during the title matches he made at least 18 goals for United. If that's struggling, I'll have a few more players doing the same thing, please.

Back for good

Maybe Lee didn't recognise the contribution he made, but I did otherwise he wouldn't have been in the side. I was always impressed that he worked like a trojan, fully committed to doing a grafting and effective team job. He invariably supplies the cross that strikers plead for from the heavens. They arrive at the right height, at perfect speed, and with the bend to deceive defenders. There might be better dead-ball merchants, but on the run Lee is the best supplier of a cross ball in the Premiership. For the time being, he represents a very serious threat on the wing to any team in the nation, but when he arrived we didn't know where he was going to finish up in the positional sense. He was a scrawny little kid then, but it was easy to see he would develop into a power-house because of his physical frame. So he went in at left back, played wide as a hard working left-winger and also tucked into the park a little to do a different job.

That's where he differed from Ryan Giggs. You knew with Ryan the potential to put on muscle strength and weight was limited. He was always destined to be a lithe, agile, electric type of footballer. But Sharpe has wonderful pace and while he has that in freely available supply, he will stay as the wonder of the wing. The options, though, are waiting later in his career to step back to full back or even seize a job in central midfield. He is a multi-purpose player. Okay, Lee doesn't have the seat-raising tricks of someone like Giggs, but he has a fantastic build for

a footballer, a natural athlete. And the learning process hasn't stopped yet. Even in the last year he has developed his all-round game, sharpened up his passing, and he looks certain to be an established figure in any England team.

Once he might have been dismissed as just a flyer, but he has added the extras that every top footballer needs, and has even successfully coped with the emergence of Giggs. Remember, before Sharpe suffered so much misfortune with illness and injury, he was *the* wonder boy. While he was out, Ryan romped on to centre stage and that might have been a terrible ego buster for some players. But not Lee. There will be other challenges for him to combat, like the progress of young Ben Thornley. No question, he is going to be a top player and that most likely means a little more team tinkering for me in the future. But for the present, Sharpe's own innermost belief must be that he has beaten the clock and is now back in the form that forged his reputation in 1990. He claimed

Lee Sharpe - "certain to be an established figure in any England team"

more than a dozen goals that season and the encouraging signs are that he can repeat the achievement on a regular basis.

Older players always know their capabilities. But the relative rookies at every club are better off being set a target. That's the easiest way to monitor their progress. Last season Giggs was two short of the fifteen goal bull's-eye I fixed for him. This is the time for him to stretch himself further and reach for it in the present season. Sharpe's finishing potential is somewhere in the same region and if they both deliver, then we will really be in business.

Keeping an old pro sweet

Bryan Robson, of course, is at the opposite end of a football career, but once the title was sealed I knew what we had to do for him. Without any shadow of doubt in my mind, we had to offer him a new one-year contract. It wasn't drafted out of charity, but management necessity. I will concede, though, if we had finished second again, the decision could well have been vastly different. Not just for Robbo, but for other players as well. I'm not certain some could have handled the emotional trauma of another failure. We might have been forced to change the team around again. It must be remembered there was incredible emotion attached to the achievement at United. Blowing it two years on the trot might have just been too much to take. With the success established on the record, we have witnessed the emergence of a strong, resilient side, full of character as well, that carries my conviction of being able to make a long-term impact on our national game. And that's why Robson had to stay.

In the post-championship season, I bent his ear so many times in beseeching one more effort from him. The request was pretty basic. "Just play for United 25 times, you old codger, and be brilliant for us," I begged Bryan. "Why the hell do you want to play sixty at half pace? " But it was almost impossible getting the message through even on the approach to his 37th birthday. He wasn't tuned in to accept that there was no fully secured first team place for him, week in and week out. For Bryan, there was only the inner knowledge that he was fitter than he had been for three years and his upfront stance with me was just as simple: "You must have some ruddy world-beaters if I can't get a regular game." That was the mental process placed in front of a very proud athlete; a question of time moving on.

In the title pursuit, though, Robbo's attitude was impeccable. During that period I kept tormenting myself with the opinion that I must try and feed him back into the team after all the injury troubles. I convinced myself the final six games would amount to the most important Bryan had ever played at United. In the event, he was six times a substitute and even from the bench he made an extremely significant contribution to the cause. Because I always knew there was somebody there to steady the rudder. He was always the player to be pushed into the action to settle the team, provide inspiration or draw out that little bit extra. He was the 999 man in our moment of need. Only the fear that I might unhinge the team's balance stopped me from playing him as much as I really wanted.

999 man

Bryan Robson - "a very proud athlete"

Coventry, in the final month, was a classic example. I wasn't happy with the state of the pitch and believed we could give ourselves a greater chance by sitting him in front of the back four. "Do you really think you should change it?" was Bryan's first question. His belief was that a successful team should be left alone. But I reminded him: "I am prepared to alter things because you are so important to us. I don't want you sitting on the bench thinking that you are not a man who matters to this club. I don't want you believing you are parked out there because you are Bryan Robson - and just to guarantee you a championship medal. I want you to feel you are playing a major part in winning the League." He said he appreciated my concern, but we shouldn't meddle with the team system at that stage and he would stay as sub. If anybody believed that Robbo's place on the bench was an act of sentimentality or tokenism, that should set them right.

It was a measure of the man that, after waiting more than a decade to win the premier title, he was prepared to sacrifice his own priorities for the team. Only truly outstanding players are able to be as clinically objective as that. He wasn't indicating to me that he considered his playing days were over by any stretch of the imagination. His conclusion was: "Let's just leave well alone, win the League and think about me later." A noble gesture, indeed. Because you have to say that, after all the supporters who had waited 26 years for football history to turn our way, the next in line for special recognition had to be Robson. More than anyone he epitomised the desire and ambition of United in landing this trophy; twelve years of magnificent endeavour and more injuries than a stuntman as his personal price.

A lion of a player Genuinely, he has not achieved all he might have done because of the busted bones and torn apart muscles he was prepared to endure for the overall club cause. For instance, if he had not been hurt during the '84/'85 campaign, United would have been champions that season. The stature of the team now is such that we don't need to depend so heavily on one player. The quality of the squad and the responsibility of each player is such that we can juggle our resources without suffering. For four or five years I believe United carried the dangerous handicap of pinning so much emphasis on a single player, no matter how huge his presence. Without Robbo, the team could appear like a wounded racing pigeon attempting to compete on one wing. That entrenched mental attitude had to be changed and I am sure the emergence of Ince was the major factor.

Because of Robson's well renowned fearless approach, he was bound to collect more injuries than most. He never sensed danger and that's what has always made him so formidable an opponent. He made his name on being a lion of a player; he scored goals beyond the capability of most players because of his courage. It made his reputation and he built his whole career on the unflinching, have-a-go instinct with which he was born. Count up the rewards - 96 England caps that might have been 150, medals from the League and in cups at home and abroad, captaining both club and country - and then count the cost. Bryan, let me assure you all, considers it a pretty fair rate of exchange. He reached for the stars and they knew he was one of the blessed.

Even when he quit with England a couple of years ago, he was still desperate to represent his country. But when he was asked to play against the Republic of Ireland at Wembley in a brand new left-sided role, he suspected he was surplus to requirements. His was a central midfield responsibility, the combative area he had dominated all over the world, and he felt he shouldn't be asked to prove himself somewhere else at that stage of his international career. Deep down, that was the major part of his decision to finish, although he always felt his best days were spent under Bobby Robson. They had a fantastic manager-captain relationship.

When Graham Taylor took over, he felt he wasn't going to skipper England again. Someone else was destined for that prized job, no more was it to be long-established Robbo. He was a short-term option for Graham and, with the writing on the wall, Bryan decided to bow out with the kind of dignity that everybody applauded. One day that final step will be taken with United, we all appreciate that, but I want a few more matches out of the cussed old warrior before he chucks his boots in the corner with us.

"We are one of the best teams in the world. Let's hope we all have plenty to cheer about in United's final decade of this century."

CHAPTER TEN

My Champions

I won't ever forget the contribution of all my champions. They were a breed apart in that fabulous season, every single one of them made his lasting mark on this club's history and tradition. From one to eleven, subs and all, I cannot praise their efforts highly enough.

Cantona was the catalyst, Giggs the newest idol, and Ince a mighty man in midfield. But there were so many other footballers of great importance, maybe hidden slightly by the headline heroes. Now is their turn for a spin in the spotlight as I reflect on a season that demanded such collective effort. Never had so few given so much for so many. Think I've heard that somewhere before but, anyway, here's my own judgement on the class of '93.

I had better start at the back with *PETER SCHMEICHEL.* He might belt me if I didn't! Well, you all know what the big Dane is like. He is daft as a brush at times; he thinks he is a centre-forward. But so many goalkeepers have that eccentric make-up about them. Off the field, Peter's an articulate, intelligent guy who likes to educate himself. He's a wonderful pianist who I understand can play a few other instruments - including the fiddle! So I don't quite understand what gets into him on the park. He can't come off without having a barney with Steve Bruce. They're like a couple of old fishwives in the 18-yard box, giving each other ear-ache. Unless they have a row I don't think they can go home and talk to the missus properly.

When it comes down to the serious stuff, though, Peter is such an outstanding 'keeper of well-established world status. Normally, British football experience and the old gut feeling tells you to leave foreign 'keepers strictly alone for our game. But he was always in a different category. I tried to sign the big man the year before he arrived at United. Brondby simply wanted too much and we

Peter Schmeichel - "magic hands"

stood back aware that his contract ran out the following summer. To satisfy myself about him, I sent the expert Alan Hodgkinson across to Denmark to watch him four or five times in different types of games and conditions. He reckoned Peter would become a giant in England and now, at a cost of £500,000 for a goalkeeper, I believe we have the buy of the century.

He is just class, lightning quick and with a watch-it presence about him. And then there is the sheer physical stature of Schmeichel. It's terrifying. If you are a striker and see him coming there's only one prayer: "Let me out of here, I'm going to get murdered." The man's a Viking, six feet four and sixteen stone. I have always boasted that there is no player who has ever dreamt of attacking me as a manager for all the times I have lost my temper in dressing-rooms around the world. But, if ever that happens, by Christ I hope it's not Schmeichel who

tries me out. Luckily, he is quite a nice guy and we would like him to hang around for a long time yet.

Bit by little bit, he has adjusted to the different pressures and demands of life in the Premiership. We saw in his early training work-outs that he had magic hands and taking crosses was never a problem for him. But it was the machine-gun rapidity of them in our game that he had to figure out and learn to combat. It was all so fast and furious for him because that was not the kind of hurly-burly football in which he learned to play. In his early matches I remember him committing himself totally against Leeds and losing out; something similar happened against Wimbledon and once more he was embarrassed. But he is now in a special category. I recall Bill Shankly's assertion some years ago that Ray Clemence saved Liverpool twelve points a season on his ability alone. Peter does that for us now.

In Denmark they idolise him. I was in the stadium when they won the European championships against all the expert opinion. You could see he was his country's king in the football sense. With us, because we have so many major

At home...

On the seventeenth with son Mark

Sinking a few at home

Relaxing with Scooter and Wriggly

Balancing the ingredients - a bit like managing United!

The pleasure & the pain...

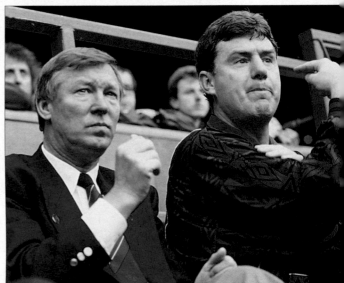

Champions!

players, it's not quite the same. But I still deliberately go out of my way to assure Peter he is in a class of his own before each game. "Hey, big man, we need a clean sheet from you today." He just nods, but clearly understands the hidden message from me. The stastitics underline every word: in two seasons he has let in 84 goals in 65 games. At least twenty shut-outs in a campaign is always another target he achieves without too much difficulty. That is the career record of a champion.

Part of the protection in front him is provided by *PAUL PARKER*. He is firmly set and an integral member of one of the most solid back fours in football. Paul's arrival at United in the summer of 1990 was courtesy of Robbo and the feedback that is so often valuable from international squad gatherings. For ages our chief scout Les Kershaw had cajoled me into signing Parker, but I held off because he was operating as a centre-back at the time and his lack of inches planted a significant doubt in my mind. His spring, the natural ability to climb higher than anyone else in clearing a cross, was unbelievable, mind you, so I decided a second opinion might be helpful. That's when I spoke to Robson. His answer was uneqivocal: "Gaffer, you have got to buy him." One issue resolved, but there

Paul Parker - "a toughie, hard as nails"

was another problem presented to us almost immediately. Parker went off and signed a five year contract at QPR. For a while his name was dropped into the pending tray.

The transfer, in fact, was only triggered about a year later when I picked up a newspaper on a pre-season trip to Sweden. Paul was reported to be having signing talks with Everton. He was our man within 48 hours and we caught everybody by surprise with the swiftness of the negotiations. But the equation was simple enough for me: he was English, we were off into Europe with the new foreign player restrictions on football's agenda, and he was a versatile player for different positions. The money bought us a lot of valuable footballer.

Since Paul moved north from his native London, we have exploited his adaptability in a triple centre-back system, but now he is settled as the right back. He was unsure about the role at first, reluctant to get forward or attempt the constructive pass. But always he was a fantastic defender because of phenomenal recovery pace. I feel when somebody is taking him on in the last third of the field, there isn't a problem that Parks can't handle. We don't lose too many when he is playing. And he has proved, even at 29, that a player never fails to move up the learning curve. His offensive passing game is good and, in training at least, he can score a goal or two.

The great management knack with Paul has always been in maintaining his level of confidence. You can't boot everybody up the backside to get a result; some need the soothing word. He is one of them, a player desperately in need of praise far more than criticism. And on that topic the United coaching staff has needed to help Paul cope with the disappointment and frustration of being dropped from England's squad in the World Cup qualifiers. We have all reminded him that it was not a damning judgement on his ability at international level, but down to other factors beyond his control. He is one of those players never really noticed because he is so good and efficient at his job. The lad's a toughie, hard as nails, and he went right through the championship season and beyond without missing a game. Consistency of performance and appearance are key words.

Consistency is also the epitome of his full back partner, *DENIS IRWIN*. He made certain there was never any silliness in our defensive play and, in my book at least, gave only one mediocre performance in 48 matches, as well as chipping in with five extremely useful goals in the championship. Mostly I marked him on an impeccable rating of nine out of ten. With so many international big-hitters in the United squad, the under-rated players sometimes tend to be overshadowed. But I know the measure of Irwin's highly productive game. Let me say if Ince was the fulcrum of our form, Cantona was the man who made all the difference, and Giggs represented a breath of fresh air, then Denis was United's Mr. Consistency. Even Incey might agree with that! He was almost faultless and yet when, towards the end of the season, they announced the PFA team awards, not one of our back four got a mention. I couldn't believe it.

For his country, the Republic of Ireland, he is played at right back while I prefer him on the other side. In doing that he has ousted three players who in very different ways had magnificent seasons for us at left back. Sharpe played there in his first season with the club, then Lee Martin had a spectacular run in the FA Cup year, only to be followed by Clayton Blackmore as we lifted the European Cup Winners' Cup. Since Denis emerged, two of them, both very good players as well, have occupied the shadows to a large degree. But he is now one of the first names on the sheet. He never says boo to a goose, a quiet lad who does his training and then is away, but he is also a durable player, able to ignore the pain and play with an injury. Irwin, and I have no hesitation in making this statement, is one of the finest full backs in world football.

I'm just as confident in the declaration that *GARY PALLISTER* is now the king of England in any assessment of contemporary centre-backs. When we bought him, it was a case of investing in raw potential with the idea of getting our money's worth long-term. But I know a lot of people pointed doubtful fingers in my direction at the time and muttered: "What the hell is he playing at?" At £2.3 million for a defender, Pally was a gamble when he joined United; just a big, raw-boned boy without any real muscle on him. The decision was taken, after we identified and assessed his make-up as a player, that there was only one course to take. We had to develop his body to make certain he was physically capable of handling the roughest and toughest in the League. So we put him on a

Schwarzenegger routine of weight training in providing him with upper body strength and, in the process, we created a monster!

There is an extra one-and-a-half stone piled on Gary since he was at Middlesbrough and, at six feet four, Pally now punches his weight. He is as strong as a bull and has extra stamina that was missing before. The calculated transfer risk - and that's exactly what it was with the record-sized fee we forked out - has paid off. He is a defensive goliath, has electric pace and can pass the ball. What more can you can ask for from a centre-half? But, I make the public promise, that what we have seen so far is only the tip of the iceberg with this feller. He is going to get better and better... that is, if I allow him to stick around! Because he drives me crackers at times with his easy-going lifestyle. Big Gary is so laid-back he almost falls over.

Gary Pallister - "the original Mars bar, crisps and Coca Cola kid"

The original Mars bar, crisps and Coca Cola kid, Gazza has got nothing on him. It must be that Geordie air that gets to them, I think. But I have been around to Pally's place and witnessed it for myself; the giant Coke bottle sitting by the telly, the family-size crisp packet meant for him alone, and the mandatory box of Mars bars. If I could get near him, I would crucify him for it. But that's only one side of his nature. Just the opposite is the emergence in Gary of that crucial competitive edge, the meaner streak that turns you into a winner. When he is revved up there's nobody better; he's the finest central defender in Britain. I accept that Des Walker was a mighty operator in his days at Forest, but Pally has so much more still to offer us. Even at 27, he is looking classier all the time. We bought the material, shaped and moulded it, and now he should be United's and England's centre-back until his mid-thirties.

His defensive partner, *STEVE BRUCE*, should have been granted international recognition as well. And I'm the witness to prove it. At the tail end of 1992, we made a trip to Portugal to play Benfica in a sentimental return to mark our European Cup Final victory over them. Out there we bumped into Bobby Robson, back in club management in Portugal, and almost the first words he uttered were to Brucie. "I made a mistake with you, son," Bobby told him. "I should have had you in my England team long before I finished." He didn't have to say anything, it was his secret anyway, but I believe that admission from Bobby carried the whole truth about his fellow Geordie. He should certainly have represented his country at the highest level; unquestionably he has been good enough. Look at it this way and just remember the international employment Jack Charlton gave Kevin Moran and Mick McCarthy. The three of them, Bruce included, have almost identical qualities and the two Irishmen actually played in the World Cup finals. There's the complete answer to the Bruce for England campaign.

It would have been fun digging out their pet nicknames if Steve had made it alongside Pally. They are known in the club as Daisy and Dolly and they even call themselves that now. Gary has been labelled because of Dolly Daydream and and, consequently, Brucie got tagged with the other title. They take it as all part of the dressing-room banter and don't get too upset about it. Brucie, anyway, is the original nice guy and a player of many parts that individually don't count for much. But if any footballer has made himself into a top-class performer on a heart the size of a dustbin lid, it's this man. All his playing assets, as I have indicated, wouldn't guarantee him a place in the big league, but Steve's bubbly personality, love of the game and incredible will to win have transformed him into a brilliant centre-back for United.

He showed that ingrained he-man quality many times in the championship season. From scoring a penalty at Middlesbrough in October, he didn't hit the net again until that amazing double against Sheffield Wednesday that placed our fingertips on the title. Now, that is a man you want on your side. He is the perfect example for the ordinary guy to copy. You don't need talent to be a millionaire, or be blessed with a boffin's brains to succeed in business. What you need is desire and Brucie has more of that than almost any other individual I have even known. He reckons he was a centre-forward once who scored with a 40-yard shot at Swansea. I don't believe a word of it - not without the photographic proof he has continually failed to provide. But I don't have any qualms with the conclusion that he has built himself into an outstanding defender, mainly because of his determination and will to succeed.

There is also a quietly maintained and steely resolve about *BRIAN McCLAIR*. He was my first major signing and the principal reason why I take so much verbal flak in our dressing-room. The other players give me terrible stick with the accusation that Choccy is my adopted son, my United favourite, and all tied up in the Scottish connection. But, as they say in that TV programme "Through the Keyhole", let's look at the evidence. McClair cost me £850,000; in six years with the club he has averaged twenty goals a season, he rarely suffers an injury and never misses a training session. I rest my case. What more can you want from a footballer? Furthermore, he doesn't moan or groan and mope about the place if I drop him from the team. Not like some of the grumpy-heads we have at United.

His championship contribution from midfield was a high level of performance and nine goals. Yet when we launched our defence of the title, I had to leave him out of the team. In fact, he has suffered from the squad competition more than even Robson; at least Robbo has benefited from the protection of being used in the European Cup. At the age of 29, seven years younger than Robbo, Brian is entitled to ask what is now in store for him at United. To resolve the question of his future, I immediately opened discussions with him on a four-year contract. That was to emphasise the point of McClair's long-term value to us. Not only can he play any number of team roles, he also has the athleticism and natural fitness that must guarantee his playing life well into his thirties. It wouldn't surprise me if Choccy is able to survive as a top player even longer than Robbo.

The issue with *ANDREI KANCHELSKIS* at the end of the championship was whether he was content to stay for a few weeks, never mind a few years. He was very unhappy at the time because he felt that his ability hadn't been appreciated enough and his place in the team wasn't secure. I could understand Andrei's dilemma. He was deeply concerned that if his club career did not progress with us, his place in Russia's squad for the World Cup might be jeopardised as well. The other consideration, obviously, was the huge changes that had been made in his life in a dramatically short time. His arrival from Donetsk, hardly one of the household names in the world game, to United was a major step for a start. Andrei then had to learn a new language - remember the problems our boys have in Italy for example - and his young wife was unfortunate enough to suffer a miscarriage. All these factors must have weighed heavily on the player's mind.

My clear duty was to try and reassure Andrei. I explained that it would be very easy for us to let him depart to another club, either in this country or abroad, and put the money in the bank. That was the quick solution. But I felt at the time, and still do for that matter, that the longer he stays in the English game the more effective a footballer he is going to be. Andrei has natural assets that merely demand fine-tuning. He has a cruiserweight's shoulders so you can't bounce him off the ball, as well as fantastic acceleration to escape defenders. The man is a whirlwind. In training sessions, his finishing is devastating and that's one area he must

Andrei Kanchelskis - "a whirlwind"

improve in competitive conditions. He must lift his head more, too, instead of just burrowing forward on lone attacks because his crosses cause a lot of damage. But, within the overall framework of Andrei's game, they are minor points we know are easily rectified. I just hope he stays at this club for a few more years because then we will undoubtedly see the best of him in first team action. He knows that already; I told him so when he wanted to leave last summer.

MARK HUGHES, remember, was another major player who left Old Trafford briefly and, in some ways at least, regretted the decision. His excursion abroad to Barcelona and Bayern Munich ended when we bought him back for £1.6 million in 1988. I have got to confess that I don't really understand why he was sold in the first place and I made it my business to tempt him back within a few months of being appointed as the manager. Since his return he has become an idol of the terraces, a latter-day replacement for Denis Law in that sense, and a footballer following the United lineage of great centre-forwards like Tommy Taylor and Jack Rowley. He has copied them in the scoring of spectacular goals. If Sparky managed a couple of tap-ins on the trot it would amount to a minor miracle. They are simply not part of his repertoire.

The way he survives nasty injuries, and barely misses a fixture, leaves everybody at the club with the impression that he must be armour-plated. His hardness and willingness to compete up the middle on his own, never shrinking from the most punishing markers, is often like waving a flag of commitment for the rest of the team. All the players understand that when they play the ball forward for Mark to hold while they support, he's not going to lose it in a hurry. But the public perception of him is just the opposite of the private person, which is unusual in football. You don't normally see a player leave his true character behind in the dressing-room; what you see on the field in the player's style of play is what he is. With Sparky that's definitely not the case. The flamboyant star is really a very quiet guy who prefers to head away from the bright lights and see his family in Wales. The terror of defences turns into a mild-mannered country gent.

The only time he ever gets grumpy with me is when he is not in the first team. And then does he get grumpy. He is like a bear with a sore head for about three weeks, murder to have around the place in fact. He regards the axe as an insult. It is too much for his personal pride to withstand such treatment and he is really upset and angry about it. I have spent time trying to explain, patiently going into the reasons and details of my decision, but it never seems to sink in with Sparky. He doesn't want explanations, just to wear his No. 10 shirt, and that's fair enough. Fortunately for me, he doesn't suffer the squeeze too often.

Mike Phelan - "fit as a flea"

The Burnley Cowboy is very different in his approach. That's my name for *MIKE PHELAN* and he is fully prepared to fulfil the adaptable role within the squad. Like all versatile footballers he may well have been handicapped from time to time by that, but it shouldn't be forgotten that Mike has collected every Cup medal with us. In the League Cup against Forest, for instance, he carried out a very disciplined man-marking duty on Roy Keane that went a long way to winning us the Wembley Final. He did that job so well because he has a very good understanding of the modern game. Ask him to do anything in the team's cause and there is never a murmur of protest. He just gets on with it. Eventually, I believe he will have a very healthy future on the coaching side of the game. He knows what he is talking about and, crucially, has the knack of getting his message across to others. But his playing days are far from finished. He is as fit as a flea and I suspect he will still be around at 36 or 37.

DION DUBLIN, in sharp contrast, might have been finished almost before he started at our club. The injury he suffered against Palace, although a pure accident involving Eric Young, was a real bad one. It could easily have ended his career. But he showed tremendous resilience and strength of character in coping with it and Dion hasn't shirked a tackle since. I make a point of that because many seriously injured players are never able to handle the trauma of their accident on returning to football. There is invariably a fear in their play and they are less effective. But that hasn't happened with Dublin. I feel certain he will make a useful contribution to United's succes in the seasons ahead.

My own son *DARREN* made it plain to me some time ago that his own career must be shaped and developed away from the club. I understood his standpoint. He naturally found difficulties because of the close family link in dealing with the problem of being out of the side. It was better for both parties, he figured, if he moved on. But, in the early phase of the championship, he was an integral part of the midfield. He played sixteen games before a damaged hamstring put him out of action. But I must admit there was a huge amount of parental pride and satisfaction for me when Darren collected his League medal.

Back-up men like *LEE MARTIN* and *CLAYTON BLACKMORE* also deserve full credit. They are both consistent and the kind of odd job men you must have in any successful camp. They have adapted to the squad system and accept their role within it. You don't face any tantrums or screaming from their sort and that helps me enormously in the smooth running of the first team set-up. One or two rebels can make certain the whole place collapses in chaos and it ends up like living in tip-toe land. That's it, the penny's dropped now, that's where MAD-DOG SEALEY must come from. Actually, I'm joking, Les, honest I am. Because our No. 2 goalkeeper has always been a brilliant guy to have in the buidling. He's the dressing-room cheerleader, always convincing the lads we are the greatest team in the world. Let's hope we all have plenty to cheer about in United's final decade of this century.

"People prattle on about our success or my track record of winning most of soccer's major prizes, but what does all that mean this morning? Absolutely nothing. I won't be happy unless the winning ways continue."

CHAPTER ELEVEN

A Job For Life

I have a clear-eyed vision of the future for Manchester United and myself that spans the nineties and stretches past the year 2000. But whether it is ever realised is extremely difficult even for me to predict. So many outside influences, decisions and policies beyond my control, are constructed within the equation. But what I do firmly undertake and promise is the personal commitment to drive foward my ambitions for the club and a management career that is, as yet, far from fulfilled. The championship is now for nostalgic fans to celebrate and occupy their conversation long into the winter nights. For me it is a dead issue, over and forgotten.

Professionally, I have to be pragmatic in dealing with the summer of adulation and glory that surrounded the achievement at Old Trafford. The League title, it must be understood, guarantees me nothing whatsoever except a place in history. It doesn't assure me of a ten-year contract or a trophy every year I'm in charge, although the latter is the fundamental, all-important driving force in shaping the seasons to come. But, at this stage, I have another singular conclusion fixed in my mind: I just cannot see myself ever being in charge of any other club, in Britain or abroad. The determination now is to finish my management life at United and, I hope, that parting is still many years away.

But I have no dangerously romantic illusions about the football business. You never know what unforeseen situation might be waiting to mug you around the next corner. It's always a highly unpredictable and risky occupation. You can never forecast, for instance, how directors react to success. I'm not referring to the United boardroom, either, because they have always been very supportive. But as a novice manager at St. Mirren, still in my early thirties, I experienced the perils of directors' being carried away by the winning game. It was a vital lesson in life for me: don't dream too long or you end up falling out of bed with a terrible bump. So I am never going to be complacent about my future in the game.

But what I do hope and pray for is some kind of productive role at United, maybe for the rest of my working days. I know the chairman, Martin Edwards, has talked publicly about what has been called the formation of a Fergie Dynasty; the kind of home-based regime centred on club personnel that our great rivals Liverpool developed to dominate the game. I haven't really talked the idea through with him, but I fully appreciate the benefits in exploiting the knowledge of a manager who understands the huge demands and special ways of United. If I had to move upstairs to help the club then, naturally, I would be prepared to do so. There will come a period when that happens, anyway.

Sooner or later, a younger, energetic and conscientious candidate to manage United is bound to emerge. When the day dawns I believe I will know precisely the qualities he should have. No names, but I can think of one or two likely lads with the potential to carry on United's development, and I don't think by necessity it must be an individual who has played or established himself with us. If I am still here in a different role, that wouldn't be an insurmountable problem. He could steer the ship while I helped to plot the course. And it certainly wouldn't be as rough or storm-ridden as when I arrived. A major sea change was inevitable at that time in 1986 and it wasn't easy to cope with the learning curve at a club where I had to absorb so many lessons as I went along. I coped on instinct, really, calling the shots I believed to be right, but wrong decisions were inevitable, I suppose. Up to seven or eight moves I made in that period proved later to be ill-advised. Nothing major, of course, but if I were overlooking the management side in the future it would be far easier nudging the new man in the right direction.

Everything I did at that time was a possible time bomb of a threat that might tick away for months, even years, before it exploded in my face. I was under the severest scrutiny, from the players, the board, the fans, the sporting public in general, and outside critics in abundance. It was judgement day, every day. I would be able to cushion my eventual successor from all of that, purely because I have experienced something very similar in the past. And, I might add, escaped from a few man-traps along the way as well. The vulnerability of it all, the empire building that goes on around you, the dramatic highs and lows of being the boss of what I consider a unique sporting institution. Now I'm certain the

Judgement day, every day

foundations of United in the nineties are not going to slip and crumble, because I won't allow that to happen. For the next man in the management chair it's bound to be a lot more secure.

Even with a guiding hand, though, I don't think it is a task for a high-flyer just leaving the playing side. It's essential for him to have some knowledge of the management responsibilities because in at the deep end there is not much margin for error. There is, admittedly, a fair degree of patience with United's directors compared with other major clubs, but you still need some insurance and that only comes from hands-on experience. Often painfully learned, too. Players are sheltered from the realities of life. They are in a cocoon of relative peace all the time. To walk straight in to the United job would be just too much to take. You have to be battle-hardened to the pressures and know instantly how to handle yourself in unexpected situations. Tactics on how to deal with the media, would you believe, are all part of life for me at United. It would be an absolute minefield for a novice.

"I have a clear-eyed vision of the future for Manchester United that stretches past the year 2000."

I am also convinced that a club of United's stature, by the very nature of the place, needs an older person patrolling the management corridors. When I see Sir Matt Busby strolling around the place, he seems to bring a calming influence without even saying a word. His presence is enough; proof of what United is really all about with an extra element of wisdom and security as well. Sir Matt, of course, has been on the board in the past, so his knowledge has always filtered down from the highest level. I won't pre-empt any future possibilities by talking about taking on the director's role because that decision doesn't rest with me. But I certainly like to think I would have a job for life if I wanted it at United. My greatest wish is to shape the whole future of the club beyond being just the manager. I declare that ambition now with one telling qualification: that I have never expected anything for nothing and won't ever take anything for granted. I believe I have worked hard for all my rewards and achievements so I might as well carry on with the well-trusted Fergie philosophy right to the end.

Just so long as the doctor says it's okay, of course, because football management is a tough and demanding business. I appreciate that slogging your guts out in the shipyards or darkening your life down a pit are also jobs full of pressures and health risks. But for all the glamour and high-profile attention of my work, the essential part is taking care of yourself. I had a recent medical and I was assured I was so perfect they could export me!

Last orders? Seriously, though, I believe there was a lesson for all of us in Brian Clough's decision to retire at Forest. When I saw the state Cloughie was in, so tired and exhausted by it all, I really felt for him. It was a time for me to wonder about myself, too. How this management life can have a devastating impact, tearing people apart, unless the danger signals are understood and obeyed. For Brian to be relegated in his final season, after all he offered to the game, was nothing less than an insult.

Only eighteen months earlier we played Forest in the League Cup Final at Wembley and if anyone had suggested the fate waiting to smack Cloughie in the teeth then, I would have laughed in their face. It didn't seem possible. But there lies the lesson for us all. If you don't keep that combative edge you are doomed. The key word is progression in football and I suspect Brian simply forgot it, until it was too late. He stopped buying new players, failed to fuel the essential competitive side of our job, and it all ended very cruelly for him. In that episode there is a reminder for everyone at our club that we must press ahead, always be fired by new ambitions and maybe impossible dreams. If you miss the train, the journey's over before it ever got started. And United have been guilty of that in the past.

But in strictly personal terms, Cloughie's sad departure also posed one very obvious question: "Could it happen to me? Will there come a time when I must ask myself whether it's time to go?" The issue is in judging the perfect moment to step aside. I am sure, when all the private heart-searching has been fulfilled, you must summon the staff and say: "Do you think I am now out of touch with the game?" I recall Cloughie's television interview in which he admitted he had struggled to adapt to so many changes within the framework of his job. To be specific, he meant highly intensive media demands, agents flying here, there and everywhere, and the freedom of contract that has made team planning far more of a hazardous enterprise nowadays. All of it combined to alter the structure of his day-by-day responsibilities and some of it he didn't like. I understand fully Cloughie's point of view. I have already served twenty years in management, but he was around a decade in advance of me, so the revolution automatically rumbled through his career with much more impact.

At Aberdeen I had three good years at the top, untroubled by players' contract freedom, before the bubble burst. Now you are forever casting glances over the shoulder about the threat from outside in setting up new pay deals for the stars everybody wants. For a large part of Brian's early years he didn't have to deal with any of that hassle. Many times he must have said quietly to himself: "Why can't it be like the old days when the job was so much sweeter?" I am sure now it must be one of Cloughie's greatest regrets that he stayed in the game a year too long. He talked about quitting many times, but my own hunch is that if he had gone upstairs and appointed Frank Clark as team manager, he could still be around and Forest would have survived in the Premiership. In my eyes at least, it amounted to a double tragedy for the whole of football. And I say that even though Cloughie was a prickly old so and so and we didn't always see eye to eye.

Feeling the moment

I believe you have to sense, almost react to a gut feeling, when the moment has arrived for you to go. You have to put your toe in and test the water. It's only then that you can discover whether you are still vitally tuned-in to the game and able to relate to players a generation or two younger than yourself. But, let me stress, Mr. Chairman, I don't think my time has arrived just yet! I keep my finger on the button with the assistance of Brian Kidd, who has learned and coped with his new responsibilities very well. It's not a question of going into minute detail with him every day, but he helps with all the necessary dressing-room feedback that I need to know. There is so much happening that I have what I call, in polite circles anyway, my built-in trivia deflector. That makes sure the important issues end up planted in the brain, and the rubbish is filtered out. Kiddo, I fully appreciate, is a crucial part of the Ferguson system that runs United.

I have mentioned Cloughie's unfortunate departure, but I plan to hang around for a few more years yet. People prattle on about our success or my track record of winning most of soccer's major prizes, but what does all that mean this morning? I'll tell you - absolutely nothing. It doesn't guarantee me a thing, not another trophy or even a wage packet next season. Of course, after a championship success, there is bound to be a period of security and I believe I am on safe territory. But what I demand of myself now is more than just that. I want to make certain I am never again exposed to the arduous circumstances that prevailed on my arrival at United. Mostly the support for me, on the terraces and right up top, was extremely generous. But let's just say I am determined that there will be no more weeks playing the hermit, hiding away at home because I was ashamed of United's League position or performances. I won't be happy unless the winning ways continue.

One-track mind
I seriously doubt, though, if I am capable of standing back from the game completely. I will always need the fix from football until my dying day. The Chairman has talked about the watershed age of, say, fifty five when team management might exert too much of a strain on individuals. I suspect he might be right. Although I do feel fit, mentally and physically solid, and strong in the working sense, that age is coming up fast on the rails. And in fairness to myself, knowing how much this job takes out of you, I can see myself around that time asking: "Where am I going now?" and "How much longer can I give myself doing this?" But my instincts already tell me I should know the answer before it's even asked. I know full well if I ever retired from football altogether, I would just be putting nails in my coffin lid. I don't want to present the impression of being melodramatic, but I would merely be making preparations for the biggest penalty box of all. As they say in Glasgow, I would be set for the Last Pick.

When you chuck the game, the future hinges crucially on having some outside interests. I don't have any at all. My all-consuming passion is football, always has been, always will be. I'm not a golfer, or a hill-walker, and I don't go down to the pub for a pint or a pipe ful l of peace and relaxation. I have owned a pub, it's true, but I haven't been in one since I was a very young man. So if I finished I would be wondering and worrying about what to do with the rest of my life. What could I do - go back to being a tool maker? No, my whole objective must be focused on working hard to make certain I have a job for life at United. I couldn't live without the game, it would be unbearable, the unthinkable option in fact. If I have anything to do with the arrangement, I'm here until the hearse shows up.

The mention of reaching fifty, the dreaded half-century, frightens people because they see it as having one foot in the grave. But I have been there and it's a lot easier than going to the dentist, that's for sure. A great deal depends on how you have lived your life. I recently met a few old schoolmates, most of whom have had the rough end of the deal employed in the shipyards, and some looked twice my age. I have been fortunate with both my career and my temperament. Aye, the Fergie Fury characterisation is true to a certain degree. I explode like a volcano at times and that gets rid of all the strain and tension of my own work load and pressures. It's a desperately needed release valve. Jock Stein, of course, was just the opposite. I still remember Jock, in that slow, lazy drawl of his, advising me: "Hey, son, leave the big stuff till Monday; it will be all nice and calm by then." But I could never wait another minute, never mind until Monday. It's violent emotion with me and I must release it, fast. I believe it's good for you to rid the system of all that deep down anger. Put all the cards on the table, tell the players exactly how you feel, and the next day it's all a different, wonderful world.

It might certainly have been a whole new ball game for me, abroad in fact, if I had taken up the invitations down the last decade. I was once invited for talks with Barcelona in London when they believed Terry Venables was set to pack his bags. It was Terry who approached me with the job offer in the first place, but eventually he had a change of mind and decided to stay in Spain for a little longer. Ironically, after we beat Johann Cruyff's Barcelona in the European Cup Winners' Cup in 1991, I was tapped again. This time it was Real Madrid who were reputedly interested in taking me on board. That feeler was made by an agent. All I can say is that I always knew the Barcelona offer was genuine because it was Terry who spoke to me. With the others, you just never know. But it's no longer an issue, because I have no wish now to leave Old Trafford for any coaching or management appointment in foreign football. When you are in charge at United the temptation is no longer there; it doesn't quite have the same attraction.

A whole new ball game

Nor does international management figure on my list of my priorities. It's an ideal job for somebody in their late fifties, as big Jock was when he took over Scotland. He was at the perfect age. But I relish the week long involvement of the club game and the task of running a national team couldn't give me the same buzz. And, anyway, it's ruddy freezing up there. We still have a house in Aberdeen and my wife, Cathy, talks about going back one day. "Not with me, you're not," I warn her. "I'm heading south for the sun." The truth is that I just can't really see myself leaving Manchester. I like the area, love the motorway accessibility that hurries me to so many matches very quickly, and the people are nice, friendly, earthy folk just like my native Glaswegians. It's a city at the hub of the domestic football empire. At Aberdeen I had a 140 mile drive to get to a game; here I can be at half a dozen in thirty minutes. I'm not going to trade in that deal, am I? The bottom line is that I would only leave United on a point of principle. Something would have to alter dramatically in the parameters of my duties to shift me. I'm not a fortune-teller, but I just don't see that ever happening.

No, the whole focus of my existence is the progress of United and the collection of a lot more silverware along the way. For instance, the record price purchase of Roy Keane was to demonstrate, and to remind the rest of football in the process, that we are not going to sit back contentedly and reflect on our glory. We definitely haven't completed our overall task. The players celebrated in style, we had a fabulous summer to dwell on the team's tremendous achievement, but now we must square up to the future with a single demand: Right, where are we aiming now, where do we aim to finish up, and how hungry are we all? I have obeyed one basic tenet throughout both my playing and management careers and that has been to forget what has gone before as soon as I've struck bull's-eye. Clear the stage, if you like, and prepare for the next act. Whatever has been achieved, at whichever club, I have the ability to shut it from my mind almost instantly. What went on last season doesn't concern me any longer, doesn't even enter my thoughts. I honestly see little point or purpose in dwelling on the glories of sport. Once it's in the bag, I must have another target to chase. The rest of the razzamatazz is strictly for our supporters and rightly so.

United:
The Next
Generation

The Keane capture was far more important to me as a professional, once the champagne hangover was all that remained of the title party. I needed to show the players that we had to retain our hunger, be mean as hell all over again. Roy, as well as being a terrific buy and a long-term asset, was my banner-carrier in getting that message across. Careful planning and intelligent manœuvring has brought United to a powerful position in the game; the next trick is to make sure the club stays there by being operated properly by the likes of me. The youth programme must be handled expertly. The championship team did us proud but, bit by little bit, the next wave of players must be presented with their own incentive for stardom. There has to be a ladder of progress, a clear indication from me to the younger element that the corner is there to be turned. In just one summer I have seen them pack their holiday bags as nine-stone weaklings and return as full-grown men. Big and bold they are, but blessed with true ability, an outstanding crop of teenagers waiting for me to plant them in the big league.

The requirement from Kiddo, the coaching staff and myself is that this successful operation doesn't snarl-up in the final phase. We have created so much and now everything must be smoothly put in place. With the European Cup on the agenda I have explained to all of them the need for patience. But already I have taken the likes of Nicky Butt, Paul Scholes and Ben Thornley abroad with us to provide them with a sense of what foreign club competition is all about. But there must also be an awareness of playing fair with the back-up players in my senior squad such as Mike Phelan, Dion Dublin, Clayton Blackmore and Lee Martin. It is a juggling act of priorities to keep peace and player solidarity within the club, helped maybe with some tinkering with the team, a bit of fiddling here and there. The atmosphere has to be right and the ultimate aim is to make everybody feel important, not like outsiders looking in. Otherwise there is a very real danger the whole show comes apart. First team regulars don't need reassurance, but even somebody like Robson, a bit edgy and itchy in accepting a different United perspective on his value, welcomes the comforting arm of approval.

The club is now in a very healthy shape but, crucially, none of us must believe that it is going to last forever. Players must not be taken for granted because that's a perilous route which ends at the cliff's edge with everybody falling into the abyss. I know full well it's virtually impossible to keep everybody happy; naive, in fact, to think that all the players will remain content and satisfied and stay at the club no matter what their fate. Some will inevitably walk through the Old Trafford door in search of different opportunites. Objectively, I appreciate some people are hungrier than others and just can't wait for their chance at United. My son Darren, who kept the midfield in very effective shape during Paul Ince's injury last season, has already told me he must seek out another club to fulfil his dreams. Sure, his category of complaint was probably unique because of the family involvement, but it was still a reminder to the staff about being watchful and keeping the dressing-room in order.

Rebellions have undermined other clubs in the jostle of first team competition and we must avoid unhealthy rumblings at United. If we manage that, I am certain the next few years will bring even more success. It took a huge, collective effort to be champions, but that presented us with little more than a launch pad.

It would be lunacy now to think we have cracked it, done it all and it's all over. Think like that and we are dead. What we have is the glorious opportunity to focus the club's football aspirations for the next ten years. My prime concern is to make sure that nobody is carried away and, to be honest, I have already detected the danger signals.

As I have explained, it's perfectly understandable for United's massive support to be euphoric even now. I don't have direct contact, or control, over them anyway. Let them get

With Nelson Mandela in South Africa during pre-season training.

carried away, let them still revel in the wonderful fallout from last season because that's precisely why they make an investment in United with the weekly cash they cough up. But inside the playing staff I must be far more flint-hearted about it all. I noted one or two potential problems in the summer and I determined then to stamp them out. Wee, simple things like the players' not informing me of some of the commecial spin-offs they had arranged as part of the whole title jamboree. I don't like people ducking and diving; it's not United. The conclusion was immediate. I had to revert to my old ways, be a party pooper if you like, and deliver a few more boots up the backside. People have to be brought back to earth. And, in the long term, it's for their own benefit.

Players' reputations are won on the field, not at some commercial sideshow. Anything they achieve in life is down to that. If they ever allow outside interests to overtake the way they earn the wage packet - by playing professional football -

then they have a serious problem. It's their choice, and if they believe they have done everything, it's going to show - and they can pack their bags and move on. With that sort of attitude they won't be wanted by me and, before an individual reaches a hasty decision, there is one obvious consideration: all the big commercial incentives, arranged in the proper way, are to be earned at United. Once they leave, the great money supply is likely to become a trickle. With a major city club, the distractions and temptations for players can become a bit tiresome for the manager. I have to be on my guard all the time like a one-man protection unit.

Keeping a lid on in

If we maintain our humility, keep our success firmly under control, then I really believe we are destined to be a truly great club again. The fundamental job is playing football and winning matches, not all the razzamatazz and hangers-on. This period is so enjoyable we must all pile the wagons in a circle and make sure it can continue through the rest of this decade. I don't want anybody to be in the position where they can accuse us of being arrogant about our success. We can

With the FA Cup -"My part of the contract bargain is to aim for winning a trophy each year."

do without the Flash Harry syndrome. It's just not us. Some clubs down in London seem to pay that price for fame, but we have enough flamboyance on the pitch. That's the place to have it, not parading it in a fedora hat with not a pair of boots or ball in sight. Get the cloth caps back on again because the big movie is over and it's back to everyday reality. Let's just remember the empty champagne bottles have been dumped in the dustbin and all we need now is a friendly cup of tea. It's time we returned to being ordinary again.

My part of the contract bargain is to aim for winning a trophy each year. Sensibly, I couldn't expect much more than that and in the last four years we've hit the target. It's not in my cautious nature to suggest this club has the capacity to dominate the game for the next twenty years. Boasting is not my business. You end up being exposed in making too many false promises. The public always suss out the charlatans in our game.

Ours is a hard, cut-throat adventure with few prizes for even the best and many a rival ready to sort out the over-cocky along the route. At Aberdeen I won the double three times but the treble was always dreamland. And down in England, no question at all, the challenge is twice as hard. I spent six-and-a-half years in securing the championship, and the club was locked into 26 years of title failure before it was accomplished, so nobody kids us about the glory game. All that gritty experience and heartache teaches you not to make off-the-cuff predictions about sweeping the board, being the best in the land and all that stuff. All it does, anyway, is increase the hostility of rival teams and their supporters. Being big-headed is definitely counter productive, and rightly so. I stepped out of line once at St.

Mirren and somebody trampled all over my toes. I was 33 at the time, just in management and full of it, celebrating five wins in a row when I fell for the sucker punch. I was asked if I thought we were ready for going up. "Promotion?" I said. "We will win this League, no bother." The inevitable happened - I lost the next four games and was cut off at the knees. The lesson was sorely learned. Don't open your mouth unless you can fulfil every word. The long memory brigade are invariably waiting to strike if you get too mouthy.

Earlier in this current season there was a shuddering reminder of what over-confidence, which surfaces around a core of complacency, can do. It was the Newcastle match. The whole dressing-room was like we had been cleared for take-off to paradise. Everybody was flying and it was yap, yap, yap. Deep down I've known for a long time we at United don't ever win games with that kind of approach. Everybody kidding on and trotting out rubbish. No, our place is much better when it's real quiet, full of brooding and atmosphere. That's when I detect the silent, but deadly, intent of the players. That's when we mean business, that's when I like what I see, when we are a bunch of whispering giants. Kevin Keegan was predictably and understandably very happy with the Newcastle performance but I was fuming at my own team. I ripped into them about being just a bunch of fat cats. It seemed to be their wish, all of a sudden, to behave like Billy Bigtime. The message struck home with a vengeance. By the following Monday at Aston Villa they had really put their super-pro act back together and we won. When the players believe they have cracked it, that the game is easy, it's my job to bring them crashing back down to reality. All I have to say, is that it's tea-cup time. I don't need even to grab hold of the old dressing-room china these days. Just mention the word and the players are ducking for cover. I'm sorry to spoil the popular myth but, in truth, I haven't slung a tea cup in anger in years. The last pot-shot was at Gordon Strachan and I missed him, so I wish the wee man would stopping moaning about it.

Making an important individual sit up and take notice is just one part of management, but occasionally you must slam your foot down and halt the progress of the whole team. I noticed at Aberdeen you can hit a winning streak and the victory roll is based on only one factor, your formidable reputation and that's all. The scenario is highly dangerous. It's the point in time where I must always move in and underline the fact that my team is not winning the way it should. There is an underlying weakness, and I have the early warning system in operation at United to detect it, because it's another form of complacency. It's not the true picture, understand. The trap has really been baited and set for the day when you meet somebody who doesn't give a damn about reputations and is totally unafraid of the biggest names on the team sheet. And that's when you hit the deck with a terrible thud, because you haven't got any reserves to fall back upon. The winning game has become too easy, and, in reality, it is never that. You have forgotten the basics and that's fatal. I just pray it doesn't happen at United because there is only one solution and it's drastic. You must dismantle the team.

Obviously, my career motivation is to build and not to destroy. But I have often been asked whether it would be possible for any United manager to move into the realm of a legend like Sir Matt Busby. Or the men who dominated football at other clubs like Bill Shankly, Bill Nicholson, Jock Stein in Scotland, and, aye, he can't be left out of the company, Cloughie himself. It's a difficult question, but I believe the right answer lies buried in the fact that if you win enough trophies on a regular basis, that has a real effect on people. The public, rightly enough, creates the legend. But I also wonder whether there is room in today's game for personalities of the stature of Sir Matt and Shanks and the rest. They were great men, it's true, but football was a very different adventure in their day.

The football jungle

We now exist in a highly-charged, black-and-white, cut-throat game. There are times when you have to be brutal - and there's no better word for it, either. Moments when decisions must be delivered that crush people. In the past, when the great men were running our clubs, teams often survived a championship season on just 13 or 14 footballers. Same side every week, no hassle, no bombing players out, none of the physical pressures of the eighties and nineties. There was a calmness, a stately aspect to football, that helped my predecessors become outstanding figures. I still believe football has its great men - it's just that the goalposts have changed so much it's harder to recognise them.

To have the influence of Sir Matt and his outstanding contemporaries, you have to earn the right. Pay your dues is the expression, as I have often been told down the last two decades, in the same way that players establish their world status. I know if I keep my ambition and hunger, collect the trophies year by year over a lengthy period, then the chance remains to make a mark. Cloughie, in my opinion, already has. Even though his final, farewell moments were a bit of a tragedy, people can only have great memories of his huge input and what he brought to football. He was a pain in the neck at times, I know he was, and occasionally I was the sufferer. Sometimes he would shout silly things to his players from the line like "Stand still!" Even to this day I have never figured that one out. He was an eccentric, for sure, but that oddball aura made him special, too. Take that mask away, though, and he was a pure and simple football man whose basic philosophy was in passing the ball. I had a lot of time for his beliefs, but I wish he had gone earlier for his own sake. Maybe I'll learn from his mistake, sense the moment to go before people are shoving me towards the door. Because timing is everything in my trade.

"You don't need to be a rocket scientist to understand that Keane is a very good player. He's going to knock in at least ten goals a season and has a fire in his belly that burns at just the right temperature."

CHAPTER TWELVE

The Infinite Jigsaw

Roy Keane was arguably Cloughie's last spectacular donation to the world of football, even if he did cost us a transfer record to prise him from Forest's determined grasp. By that time Brian had quit the management scene, but he was still very much in control when Keane's name topped a dossier dropped on my desk.

It provoked, I can tell you, a major upstairs-downstairs investigation at Old Trafford that might have been lifted straight out of the annals of MI5. The reason was that, until the true facts turned up, I thought we had blundered and missed out on signing the young Irishman for not a penny piece. And that was at least two years before we frightened the bank manager to death with our £3.75 million cheque to Cloughie's old employers.

The plot thickened for me way back in the 1990-91 season when I sent Les Kershaw, United's chief scout, off to Anfield to do a detailed breakdown on Forest. The match facts weren't Les's primary concern when he arrived back and reported to me. "I have seen a player, a real player," he said. "Young lad who plays for

Forest. Keane's his name, Irish, from Cork." The alarm bells immediately started clanging in my head. "How's it we didn't know about him before they got their hands on him?" I demanded. Les couldn't give me an instant reply, but promised to find out. That's when I started the inquiry, major it was, too.

Keen on Roy

Three weeks later Roy played for Forest against us at Old Trafford. He had a blinder, Stuart Pearce bombed in a free-kick and we lost 1-0. I knew that I had seen a *real* player in Keane that day and the publicity hype was soon surrounding him as football's newest star. Not long afterwards I read an interview from him in which he explained that he had drafted a letter to every senior club in Britain begging for a chance to play. Forest were the club that moved in. Now that really did get my back up. Having focused so much attention on the creation of a wide-ranging scouting system I was upset we had missed out. Where the hell was that missing letter? I had to be provided with the answer. I also wanted to know how he had slipped through the net in Ireland as well.

Now, the mystery on the Dublin side of the water was easily solved. We have a scout based in that lovely city who monitors all the county fixtures and schoolboy representative teams whenever they hit town. Trouble was, Roy never even made the Cork kids side because he was too small. At that stage, Keane the late-developer looked as though he wasn't going to make it. So I could exonerate the scouting set-up. But what about that damn letter? I couldn't remember seeing it and the club had been turned upside down without anybody laying hands on it. When I signed Roy it was the first question I tossed at him. "Oh, that, letter," he explained. "You didn't get one. I never actually wrote to United then - because I didn't think I was good enough for you." Now that surely must be one for the Guinness Book of Records - the most expensive postscript in football history! But at least I was relieved to be presented with the truth. I couldn't have handled any outcome that indicated we had bungled it - I would have been very angry indeed. Let's just say heads might have rolled if a guilty verdict had been returned.

Calling Mr. Clough

But, first, back to Act One in the Keane saga. As soon as I had watched him perform in that match at our place I was on the phone to Mr. Clough. Needless to say, I didn't get him and ended up chatting things through with Ronnie Fenton, his second-in-command. I quickly raised the issue of buying Keane. "No way, " he warned me. "The boy's a diamond, a great player, and we are not going to be selling him." But I never quit that easily. So when Forest belled me about Neil Webb after we won the European Cup Winners' Cup, I dropped Roy's name into the conversation again. Still, the answer was no. They wouldn't entertain selling him when I made another call, either. And then, finally, when Webby did return to the Forest fold I asked about a part-exchange arrangement. Being a transfer pest, and one with money, sometimes works. Not this time. We had stalked Keane all the way, no question about it, but Cloughie was adamant and resisted our every overture.

But at the end of the championship season Keane's name was still the most prominent in our planning. We held the usual review of the campaign, scanned the next season, and decided that he was the player, above everyone else, we must have in the team. It was imperative, as far as I was concerned, even though publicly I made pointed references to European Cup qualification rules and Roy's Irish nationality. To be fair, all of that was only a con trick. Whatever the regulations on so-called foreigners, we were not going to miss out on him. No chance. But I was aware of the dangerous blind side run that Blackburn might be tempted to make. They always like to get in first, roll out the eye-boggling terms in front of a player, and shake hands as though there is then an obligation to go through with it. It's a way of putting the individual under pressure.

Once again, just as with Alan Shearer a year earlier, they lived up to the usual summer script. When Keane went for talks with Blackburn, I wasn't even aware of it because we had not been given permission by Forest to speak to him. Neither had they, as far as I am led to believe. Really they jumped the gun. Once Forest indicated they had finally decided to sell the player, Blackburn were in. I don't think Kenny Dalglish did anything wrong, but under the strictest interpretation of the League regulations he may have stepped marginally over the borderline. Kenny probably felt entitled to talk to Roy, even though his club weren't

Roy Keane in Forest strip - "a *real* player"

aware of it, once Forest made their own position on his future quite clear. To be honest, I worried about the sudden development after what had happened with Shearer in 1992. Within 24 hours I was on the phone to Frank Clark, Cloughie's successor, and received the nod to speak to Keane.

Testing the water

It was the beginning of June and he was due to go on holiday and so was I. A day or so before my plane was set to take off for the sun, I had lengthy talks with Roy. I was surprised when, as I explained how determined we were to have him on the staff, to hear him say he had always understood we weren't interested in him. He admitted, though, that Denis Irwin had told him I was on the case. My short and sweet answer was that for two years I had been banging on his manager's door. "I don't blame him for not telling you, mind you," I quickly added. "That might have caused Forest problems they could do without." Quickly I impressed on Roy that joining United would change his whole horizons. Number one, he would have a tremendous club platform in the World Cup build-up with the Republic of Ireland; two, he would be with a club whose history was littered with great Irish footballers; three, although tested at international level, there was the extra challenge in Europe of facing glamour teams like Barcelona, AC Milan and Oporto; and, finally, four, he should actually be paying me to be playing in such a fabulous stadium as Old Trafford!

I emphasised also that I carried the deep conviction we could win the League again and, with his considerable help, the European Cup would also be within our reach. With that parting shot I was off on my hols, quietly confident to be

"An outstanding competitor, with a fire in the belly that burns at just the right temperature."

sure, but naturally concerned that we hadn't got the whole deal under wraps before I left. I always prefer to tidy up transfers early in the summer, so you can head off to the beach with a clear conscience knowing the job has been done. But these days that's rarely possible and, anyway, the next phase was in the hands of the chairman, Martin Edwards. Forest told him they wanted £5 million and not a penny less, but all clubs are the same, and that was the haggling point. Our offer was £3.5 million but, while I was on my holiday, I slipped a call into Roy and immediately knew we were in business. He told me, gave his word in fact, that United was the club he intended to join. Although Arsenal were in, he didn't want even to talk to them. It was back to the sangria and suntan oil for me with a sigh of relief. For the chairman, back at home, the money game was a little more complicated with Blackburn, ourselves and Forest in a stand-off. The European signing deadline triggered our ultimately successful move. We needed Keane before the shutters went down on player qualification for the first round and, with the extra £250,000 from Brian Carey's sale to Leicester, the deal was struck at £3.75 million.

But, more than any other factor, the transfer was effectively swung by one man - Keane himself. He made a career decision, instead of a money-no-object move. The worry with Blackburn is always the money because they have bank vaults full of the stuff. Jack Walker can gazump us any time he likes, even if it hurts me to admit it. In pure financial terms, he can buy and sell any other club in the country, including United. All you hope is that the player involved takes a broader view and considers other material factors in his future, like pursuing the major trophies. Roy did that, maybe Shearer didn't, but that's all now water under the bridge. Alan made the decision he felt right for him and there is no doubt whatsoever that Keane could have collected a lot more money going to Ewood Park instead of signing for us. I hope some compensation is heading his way with the spin-off bonuses from far more trophy collecting with us than he could ever expect at Blackburn. But he was always positive about joining this club and, when he looked me in the eye, I knew I was talking to a footballer who would not break his word.

The new Robson?

You don't need to be a rocket scientist to understand that Keane is a very good player. He is an outstanding competitor, young, built like an Irish wash-house and has a marathon runner's stamina. Apart from all that, he is going to knock in at least ten goals a season and has a fire in his belly that burns at just the right temperature. He doesn't go too far on the park, but he is fully prepared to let any uppity rival know he won't be messed about. Roy can look after himself and nobody is going to bully him into submission. The peak for him is still three or four years over the horizon when maturity and experience is going to make him one hell of a player. Comparisons with Robson - and I accept being likened to another player, no matter how accomplished, can rankle anybody - are inevitable. They are so alike, particularly in the damage they do to the opposition around the penalty box. Both have enough courage for a battalion in the way they pile in for a goal, without any care for personal safety. They just throw themselves in front of a defender's boot, ready to take the personal consequences, just as long as it helps to secure a team victory.

Both have a depth of resolve and strength, physically and mentally, that makes them formidable. Sure enough, Roy at 22 must now build the little extras into his game that Robson has acquired since he was a similar age. The knack of showing patience on the ball, creating his own time and space and the concentration necessary to provide the pass that counts.   Over the seasons ahead that improvement is assured and so, I have to suspect, is the fact that Roy is going to be hurt playing a game based on boldness, bravery as well as skill. Like Robbo, he is prepared to take the punishment as a calculated risk that comes with his attacking style. But he is as tough as teak, with a fantastic physique for a young lad, and I think his resistance to injury will be better than Bryan's because of the way he is built. He is a compact, solid individual whereas Pop is strong as a bull but with a wiry frame. There's a bit more flesh on Keane to cushion him from all the painful blows.

There is that close bond in playing approach between the two of them, though. Just like our club skipper, Roy has already laid down the indisputable proof that he learns fast in the development of his own game what he is able to do for the team. I employed him in a wide role against Chelsea earlier this season and he couldn't quite come to terms with what was expected. Next trip it was the European Cup first leg at Honved and, yet again, I asked Roy to fulfil that specialist job for us. He had a blinder, as you know, and scored two superb goals. There was instant proof for me of Keane's adaptability to the team system which added to his other encouraging qualities as an all-round performer. We bought him, essentially, as a goal-scoring midfield player, a very rare diamond product in the modern game and that's why he cost so much. But he is also a utility footballer who can fill most emergencies as a full back, centre-back or up at the sharp end - something close to five players in one. I have heard Roy complain that he lacks the on-the-ball tricks to operate in certain areas, but I have a hunch he is just being over-modest. Maybe it's a subtle message to me that he wants to be hunting down the middle where he can make the runs into the box for goals, and not be stuck out on the wing. I can understand, to some degree, his argument but it's never going to be a lack of skill or vision that lets Roy down. He can look over the rainbow right now, safe in the knowledge he is going to get better and better.

Money well spent

I accept he cost the club a huge amount of money, but Keane is a great deal of football talent and well worth the investment. Remember, £2.5 million has been thrown around for a full back and these days other defenders are in that kind of price bracket. We laid out a small fortune and in return got a skilful, creative midfield player and proven match winner. United are used to beating sporting records, so it presents no problem for me holding another in the transfer market. The likelihood is that in the very near future it's going to be surpassed, anyway. Television revenue and sponsorship, coupled with a shortage of top quality players, has driven the price spiral upwards. It can be a chilling experience when the cheque book comes out and all the noughts are penned in, but I can't concern myself strictly with the money. It's not my prime domain; the players, the overall and lasting strength of the team, have to be my priorities. It used to be different when I first arrived at United, but now I bypass any impulse to carry through the soul searching and self-examination when the big money has to be spent.

I first realised I had to shut my mind to the enormity of such outlay when I involved myself in a welter of spending in the summer of '89. It had to be done as a strategic investment to maintain the status of the club and it had to be done right then. I think the high-level backing I received at the time has subsequently been fully justified. But, admittedly, I had forcibly to make myself stand away from a personal guilt complex. I did worry about lashing out so much money which our supporters had struggled to find in times of economic depression and dwindling jobs. The thought was about throwing an awful lot of their cash in one direction in, for instance, spending £3.75 million on one player; it's true that many managers are expected to buy a whole team for that. But there is a combination of factors out of my control at a club like United, number one being that the sellers always demand more at the mention of our name. Sometime soon, though, I suspect the gravy train is going to slam in the buffers - with me at the wheel.

Keane - "a goal-scoring midfield player; a very rare diamond"

I honestly believe that, if the whole transfer situation continues to get sillier and sillier, we are rapidly approaching the point where I will call a halt. The playing strength at this club is going to allow me to say a very resounding no to the crackpot inflation now threatening major football. I can certainly foresee the day when a big star, no matter how much I believed he might benefit my side, will be put beyond a self-imposed United price range. I see ominous dangers for us all in the way players' wages and fees are going way out of control, and very soon a no-further line must be drawn by the sensible people in soccer. My aim at United is to retain a level of equilibrium on all squad pay packets. We have too many stars to satisfy with high profile salaries even to be tempted into the realms that Blackburn, for example, undertake with certain principal players. I aim to make sure that there are no damaging gaps in United's pay code that might allow people to bellyache. I don't want morale-damaging splits with some moaning that they collect only half the weekly figure of a team-mate. There is also a full share-out for all from the bonus system and that adds a further balancing effect.

Balancing the books

At times in the past I have needed to walk a financial tightrope, too. And been the butt of an odd boardroom joke into the bargain. Whenever I have gone in there with the request for another sackful of transfer money, the directors, either Maurice Watkins or Mike Edelson to be precise, have usually piped up: "Alex, I suppose that this is for the last piece of the jigsaw, is it?" Damn cheek! The answer has always been, of course, "At this time, yes it is, but this is ruddy big jigsaw and we might need another lump of money in a month or so." To be exact, the jigsaw has actually cost the club £19.5 million on twenty three different players, from very small purchases to major outlays, in almost seven years. In the same period I have recouped £6.8 million, which leaves me close to £13 million adrift. Sounds like a lot, and I suppose it is, but when you calculate the sums within the great United exchequer, it adds up to less that £2 million a year. And I don't think that's too bad.

I think I can underline my own buying strategy with a little story about Steve Coppell during his days in charge at Crystal Palace. He rang me to chat over a valuation of England goalkeeper Nigel Martyn. At the time he was haggling over signing him. Steve told me that his chairman Ron Noades believed Martyn was worth no more than £800,000 and he couldn't budge the selling club at that. "They want a million," Stevie told me." What do you reckon I should do ?" I told him to put the phone down and ask his chairman: "Are Palace a big club, or are we small time?" Steve got his man for a million. You always have to take the pulse of the market and I don't think, at least in the financial madness of the last five years, that I can be branded as a big spender. At United, because of all the great expectations of the support and the media, it's a high spending road that can't be avoided. And finally I would like to rest my case with a selection of bargains we have acquired from McClair through to Cantona; the first was £850,000 and the latter £1 million. For me they were both a steal at the money. And then I think of what Ince, Pallister, Sharpe, Schmeichel and big Eric might fetch if I were ever ready to trade them in. At a guess, no less than £20 million - or more than all my spending money since I joined United.

Scrimping and saving

Mind you, I had to survive a major economic policy change to get where we are today. It was a very frugal existence for everybody at my old club, Aberdeen, where Scottish thrift ran deep and the pockets were even deeper. My chairman up there was a fabulous man, Dick Donald, and his well-kept watchword was that we must never be in the red while he was in charge of financial affairs. To underline the point, the biggest deal I ever completed at Pittodrie was for Peter Weir at £225,000 cash, plus a player, which brought the grand total to a monster quarter of a million pounds! A real bank-breaker, that one, in granite city. So on my arrival at United I was something of a Scrooge for a while. They must have thought I was a bit of an oddball with my tight housekeeping approach. I used to go spare at what I thought was a waste of resources. But the people who gave me glances that suggested I was waiting for the men in white coats didn't know my immediate past in management.

At Aberdeen, for starters, we used to travel to away matches in a local transport bus, hard-backed seats and all. Talk about television and on-board videos, this heap didn't even have a radio. To keep all the players occupied, I had to run quiz games on the long trips down to Glasgow and Edinburgh for the major matches. They were journeys that appeared to last forever. Once, in the deepest midwinter, I can remember the front window of the bus being shattered on the way across the moorlands to play Hibs. It was howling and an absolute freezing misery with the wind screaming past us down the bus. We had to stop, unload the hampers in the boot and get the tracksuits out for the lads. Then I had the players pounding up and down the gangway to keep warm. Not surprisingly it took me a while to adjust to a vastly different life at Old Trafford. For a couple of years, it was all nice and calm for the chairman. He must have viewed my management with generous optimism when I asked him for a mere two hundred and fifty grand for my first signing, Viv Anderson. Then I came back from Japan and went for broke, shelling out all the millions on the reconstruction of the present team. Better not ask him what he thinks of me now!

The final piece?

People wonder if all the mega money exploits in the transfer market are over for United, and it's a difficult question to answer. You just never know what the future is going to unfold. Brucie's approaching the veteran stage but is still looking in fine shape, Robbo is hovering on 37 and yet we might squeeze another year out of his career, and nobody knows at this stage where Giggs will finish up playing in a positional sense. They are the imponderables that only the passage of time will resolve. But my belief has always centred on the idea that the introduction of top players from outside must add a competitive sharpness to any squad. They stoke the fires, so if a world-class player emerged somewhere next week, then I know we would pursue him with a great deal of vigour and a very handy cheque book. The youth policy, though, is now primed to put the pressure on the rest. Within the next year, one or two of the younger element are going to be shaping up to the challenge to provide me with the competition for places that is the life blood of any successful outfit.

I have seven or eight kids waiting patiently for *the* opportunity, young footballers on the threshold of the big time. The argument within the game has forever been that the manager has yet to be created who can bring a whole youth team through to senior level soccer. To a point, I agree. I don't think it is possible to manoeuvre eleven through the ranks together; but, in slow stages, I believe it is the dream that can be realised. Teenage players have different phases of development in both emotional maturity and physical growing-up. You can get them half-way there in laying down the ground rules of what makes a professional; the other half is down to their own self-sacrifice and dedication. They must have pride in the job they are training to do

Stretching his legs for United against Benfica

and a fierce commitment to it. Their non-footballing pals might be out at the disco or having a Friday night pint and, if they desire to make it right to the top, they are temptations that must be ignored. Otherwise they are doomed before they start. But just think of the rewards if they are successful at United. Millions would sweat blood just for the opportunity.

Because of our very powerful first team, some people seem to believe it will have a suffocating effect on the kids. That somehow youthful ambition will be stunted. I don't agree with that standpoint, either. If the youngsters are good enough, what a challenge it must be for them to consider they could muscle aside an Ince or a Pallister or a Keane from the Premiership side. They appreciate, too, that big reputations wouldn't matter to me. If they have the quality, age is no barrier. I have proved that in the past with Sharpe, Giggs and Mark Robins jumping the senior queue at no more than eighteen. All the home-grown talent, of course, is not going to burst through at Old Trafford. You must always be careful not to choke the system, so some are going to emerge from the ranks and move on because they have narrowly failed to reach United's highest standards. But at least they have been steered in the direction to carry their careers forward, and make a healthy living in the game, at other clubs across the country.

Roy relaxing with the soaraway *Sun* - "but there are seven or eight kids waiting patiently for *the* opportunity, young footballers on the threshold of the big time"

To be honest, it's too hazardous to even hang your hat on any young footballer and guarantee the status of superstardom. Always, in the early, formative years, we are talking about potential. Character, temperament to play under the toughest demands, and dedication all come into the equation. But, with all those factors in mind, I feel pretty sure that we now have a rare bunch from last season's youth team making progess in the reserves and on the verge of the first team in the very near future.

I suspect that Nicky Butt, still only eighteen, will be the first to shoulder his way through the door, purely because he is more physically developed than the rest. In today's game, power, pace and strength are essential and Nicky has them. But he has other tremendous assets, a midfield runner who is good in the air, with a great goal sense and willingess to get in the box. He's like Robbo of almost twenty years ago. But he is not the finished article and it's going to take him three or four more years before he makes it as a real first team player. Others might make the breakthrough later, but overtake Nicky in their senior development as players.

One is Paul Scholes. He is a wonderful player who can operate in midfield or up front. Not the biggest, but a hard little nut, and not the quickest either, but what a brain. He needs to get an extra half yard and he probably will as he grows, but is already blessed with great vision. If he doesn't make it, we might as well all pack in and go home. The other likely to force his way through soon is Ben Thornley. He's a traditional winger, always hugging the line and in the sawdust. He attacks the full back, crosses magnificently, is very brave and also has the extra dimension of being a finisher. Ben's only first team problem is having the extra competition of Sharpe and Giggs already ahead of him. Another winger on the production line is, of course, Keith Gillespie, who is now farmed out with Wigan to gain valued experience. Within the next year I believe he will be capped as a full international by his country, Northern Ireland. Already he has scored a Cup goal for our first team.

There are plenty of others like David Beckham, Gary Neville and Chris Casper. You can see all the hallmarks in young Chris that he has been raised in a football family. His father, Frank, has really done a good job on him. He smoulders with the desire to be a top player, everything about him is professional. I moved him back to central defence because we had a glut of good midfield players and we couldn't afford to leave him out. He reads the game well and has good pace; what he needs now is upper body strenght to tangle effectively with the toughies of the game. His defensive partner, Gary Neville, is someone whose position could eventually be elsewhere in the side. But he is very determined and good in the air for his height. Young Beckham is well on his way, too, and has already proved he can score very important goals.

They represent my hopes and ambitions for the rest of this century, but I appreciate there wouldn't be a future at all for even a huge club like United without the one factor that makes it all possible - the fans. I genuinely marvel at their sacrifice and commitment to the club.

People power

This club is renowned for the unbelievable loyalty of the fans and I accept it's my responsibility to be the human bridge between them and United. I fully understand that they are not going to agree with every decision I make, and that they will have a grumble or two along the way, but I don't mind that if they appreciate that I am working my heart out for them.

We have hundreds of thousands of followers around the world, many scattered oceans away from Old Trafford, but others you treat almost like staff. One guy is Norman Williams who is deeply involved with a real bunch of fanatics. He is there with his pals on the half-way line for all the junior team games and on the dot for every training session. If he goes missing, Norman's wife rings to apologise and tell us: "He won't be in this week, he's got 'flu." It's almost reached the point where they send in a doctor's note if any of them are out of action. Then there's another big guy who moved his home from London just to support us. And I'll never forget the brothers from Stretford, who have now formed a pop group called Lloyd Almighty, who used to wait for me leaving the ground after every match in the early days. All they wanted to offer was genuine words of encouragement and advice to keep my chin up when life was a bit rough. Much further afield is the backing of Joe Glanville and his other United mates in Malta. There is also the London crew, Ralph Mortimer, Ian the taxi driver, Andy, Paul and Maggie. I have never known support like it; the devotion of them all is unique.

Sometimes, I suspect, the players believe I ramble on about the support too much, impressing on them the heavy cost in time and money of following United. But I deliberately take that stance because I worry that so many of the younger players don't really know what being a fan means. They have been drawn away from supporting their own clubs by the commitment to weekend schoolboy football, which has mushroomed in recent years. Not for them the scarves, fanaticism and saved-up pocket money to follow a particular team.

But I know all about that, because I was one of the Glasgow Rangers army before I became a player. I trailed them to Tottenham and Wolves in European competition, went with them to Sweden, and got crushed on the barriers of Firhill in the fifties. I used to sneak from the Cowshed at Ibrox, over the fence and into the gentlemen's enclosure to nick the enamel Bovril mugs to collect the tanner deposit on them before the police could feel my collar. And also go hunting for the screw-top beer bottles around the ground to return to the Govan pubs for the coppers you got back. Aye, I was one of the Passage 12 gang in those days and that mentality of being a terrace follower hasn't ever left me. I still try to be on the same wavelength as the fans.

Into the future

At the moment, for instance, we are at a crossroads as to what exactly the future strategy for Old Trafford should be. Now we are a plc, it's clear there must be the greatest concern for economics whether it's in buying a player or building a new stand. But my own view is that if it's possible to build a 70,000 seater stadium, then we should go for it. The face of the sporting world is changing, you see, and once again football has become respectable family entertainment. The scourge of the hooligans has largely vanished. Women are coming back to the game and once that happens, the kids come with them. We must provide the seats and the space for them to watch United if they want. The only immediate solution is to go double-decker over the top of the United Road and Scoreboard End stands. It's a project under review but the problem is that it would probably provide no more than ten to fifteen thousand extra places. So what about the unthinkable - leaving Old Trafford for a brand-new stadium on some other site? I never thought I would even consider it, but now it's a concept that has to be seriously studied as this club moves towards the next century. Maybe it's a vision twenty years into the future, but I would still like to be around then with, as they say, still more silver than Sothebys' in our boardroom.

And I'm not dreaming.